THE QUEEN'S SHILLING

Front cover photo

The boys of 'C' Company who enlisted
on 8th February 1956.

Photograph taken after basic training at Yeovil Camp.

THE QUEEN'S SHILLING

Alfred Cartwright

DB

DIADEM BOOKS

All Rights Reserved. Copyright © 2008 Alfred Cartwright

No part of this book may be reproduced or transmitted in any form or by any means, graphic, electronic, or mechanical, including photocopying, recording, taping or by any information storage or retrieval system, without the permission in writing from the publisher.

Published by Diadem Books

For information, please contact:

Diadem Books
Ocean Surf
CLASHNESSIE
IV27 4JF
Scotland UK

www.diadembooks.com

Cover design by Angus Muller

ISBN: 978-0-9559741-6-8

Dedicated to all those serving in the
Royal Army Service Corps

Table of Contents

Chapter One	1
Chapter Two	6
Chapter Three	11
Chapter Four	16
Chapter Five	23
Chapter Six	32
Chapter Seven	40
Chapter Eight	45
Chapter Nine	51
Chapter Ten	57
Chapter Eleven	66
Chapter Twelve	72
Chapter Thirteen	80
Chapter Fourteen	88
Chapter Fifteen	94
Chapter Sixteen	101
Chapter Seventeen	111

THIS IS A TRUE STORY OF THE BRITISH NATIONAL SERVICE. IT IS A STORY OF THE TRIALS AND TRIBULATIONS OF THOSE DAYS.

SET IN THE MID-FIFTIES, THE EVENTS ARE SEEN THROUGH THE EYES OF THE AUTHOR, WHO WAS SERVING IN THE ROYAL ARMY SERVICE CORPS AS A YOUNG SOLDIER.

Chapter One

It was just three days before Christmas, 1955. The previous night I had had very little sleep. My mind had been all over the place.

Arriving at work last Monday morning, Ted, our boss, had called both of us into the office.

"Look, lads," he said grimly, "this is very hard for me, but I won't beat about the bush with you. I'm going to have to let you both go. The business is being forced into liquidation—the wolves are barking at the door, so to speak."

"But Ted," I exclaimed, "business has been brisk all year! How can this be happening? We all understand how trade is in the upholstery business after Christmas—slack in January and February, but it always picks up again."

"It's no use, boys," Ted shook his head, sadly. "My business partner has been fiddling the books, lining his own pockets, you might say. That's the real truth of the matter. Look, you two, I am so sorry, but it's out of my hands, now. You can both work until the end of the week, or leave today if you both wish to do so—to start looking for new positions, like; you both know, lads, that you would be classed as improvers and damned good ones at that. Any new employer should be glad to have you and I will state that on your references. You will be paid two weeks' wages. I only wish it could have been more."

"Look Ted, we will work up until dinner time so that we can finish the three-piece suite we are working on."

It was 12.15 when we finally finished the suite. We both just looked at each other and both more or less said in unison, "Let's get ourselves a pint!"

We didn't speak more than two words from leaving the works until we had sat down in the Royal Oak with a pint. The pub was quite deserted at this time of day. Apart from John and I, there was only one elderly gentleman seated in the corner enjoying his pipe with a pint. Behind the bar the landlord stood polishing some glasses.

Settled with our pint and taking a good swig, we both looked at each other.

"Well John, what now?"

"Look Alf, I might not be continuing in the upholstery trade."

"What!" I exclaimed. "You do know what's looming around the corner? Call up! But by keeping in the trade, John, we could both get deferment until we're twenty-one."

"Look Alf, I know I have kept it pretty quiet, but the truth is I have already had my call-up papers—a few weeks ago, in fact; and the truth is, Alf, they don't want me—perforated ear drum, you know."

"You lucky sod, John! Who's been the sly one, then? But what are you going to do?"

"An uncle of mine has been pestering me for a while now—he wants me to start working in his furniture shop and train me up as a salesman, so to speak. Think I will take him up on it now. Now what about you, Alf? What's your plans?"

"As you know, John, I had hoped to finish my full apprenticeship and get deferment. But I must say, the future is now looking on the black side. To be honest, this has come as a bit of a blow. You know what it's like in the trade this time of the year. Who's going to take me on at this time? Reckon I've got until the end of January. If I don't get myself sorted out by then, it will be a case of the wolves at the door, as Ted put it! Then I suppose I'll be joining thousands of others in the ranks. Hell, what a mess!"

My tea would be ready on the table, as usual, about 6 o'clock. I had decided I wouldn't mention anything about today's revelations until after the evening meal.

I suppose I had a bit of an inkling on how Ted must have felt, because I knew how my parents had come to rely on my small contribution each week.

Dad was seated in his usual chair, filling his pipe. Now mother came out of the kitchen and settled down. I took a deep breath.

"Look, Mum and Dad, I have something I must get off my chest."

Then I related all of the day's events—of how Ted had sat me and John down in the office, how Ted had given us the bad news. After a few moments' silence, it was Dad who spoke first.

"Seemed a shifty, that one," he said. "Guess I wasn't far wrong. What puzzles me is why? Wasn't he the one who put money into the business at the start, like a 'Silent partner'—wasn't he? Reckon he must have borrowed the money to put in and hasn't been paying it back. Got himself into a load of debt like and decided to milk the business for all it was worth, then do a runner—before it all went pear-shaped, so to speak. Feathered his own nest, that one did, Alf."

Now mother spoke for the first time. "Been listening to you both. Strikes me your father seems to have hit the nail on the head regarding that one, but it's no use crying over spilt milk, is it? Have you made any decisions yourself, lad?"

"Won't be able to do much, Mother, until after Christmas is over. Everyone is packing up for the break now. Don't think I will be thinking about Christmas this year. Come January and I will be looking in earnest—had my heart set on completing my apprenticeship, I had. Just got to be patient and wait and see what evolves in the New Year."

In January I did start looking in earnest, travelling as far as Bradford, Huddersfield and of course my own town. But the answers were always the same: "Business is slack—call back in March or April, might be able to do something then, lad."

But I knew the army wouldn't hold back for me. Also, now I knew that if something didn't crop up soon, it would be the army and that was a fact.

This was the main reason why I hadn't been sleeping. However, January came and went and the inevitable had to be faced. It was time for another heart to heart with my parents.

Once again I waited until after the evening meal. Dad had lit his pipe—it was like a ritual with Dad. He chain-smoked that damned pipe from getting up until going back to bed. Yet I wouldn't have swapped him for the whole world.

Mother had now completed her chores in the kitchen and had settled herself in the dining room again.

"Look Dad, I haven't had any success on the job front—didn't expect any, really; bad timing for some bugger to cook the books! I've been doing quite a bit of soul searching this last few weeks and can only come up with one conclusion—I have decided to join up as a regular. It will mean three years instead of two. Given it a lot of thought and the extra year will be worth it. Some of my mates are already in now. One pound a week they get, Dad, and after deductions end up with just ten shillings to manage with! Being a regular means my pay will be three times that amount—three guineas, to be exact. The way I see it, Dad, I'll still be able to help you two out occasionally."

"Well, lad, I can see you've been doing your homework. When is it all going to happen, Alf? When was you thinking of going down and doing the deed?"

"Tomorrow—Wednesday. Might as well get the ball rolling, Dad."

Chapter Two

The uncertainties behind me, the future seemed suddenly more positive. On waking up, I glanced at my watch. It was 8 o'clock. I had overslept! That Wednesday morning and I felt great.

Mother was in the kitchen rustling up some breakfast. When breakfast was over I sat down and started mulling over the decisions I had made the previous day.

Dad suddenly spoke. "Decided which outfit you are going to join, son?"

"The paratroop regiment," I replied without hesitation.

"The paratroops!" my Dad exclaimed. "Don't join that mob, son!" He went on to tell me all about the paratroop regiment. "They sent six thousand of them lads, dropped them right into the enemy lines at Arnum; the idea was to soften up the 'Gerries' before the big push. Hardly any of them lads got out alive." He shook his head. "Why not join the R.A.S.C. Alf? That's the mob I was in, son. It can be a bit dicey going out to the front line, picking up the wounded, but not as risky as the para's, lad, plus you'll learn how to drive all types of vehicles. How about it, son?"

"Okay, okay!" I relented. "I wouldn't want you and mum worrying, now."

"So that's decided, son. We'll feel a bit more content now. What bus will you be catching?"

"Thought about catching the quarter to nine."

I had a rule never to sit on top of the bus. Upstairs was for smokers and it was like thick fog in those days, so I sat downstairs. At least my eyes wouldn't be watering.

I remember walking into the recruitment office. A big sergeant was seated behind the desk. He immediately stood up when he saw me coming in.

"Good morning son, have you come to join up?"

"That's right. Thinking of taking the three years stint."

"Great!" the sergeant retorted. "We don't get many of you boys wanting to sign on. Which regiment was you thinking of joining, son?"

"The R.A.S.C., same as my father."

"Good, good! The first thing we have to do is get you a medical."

Leaving the recruitment office, I was driven up to the local Duke of Wellingtons Regiment for the medical. The medical was speedily completed and before long we were driving back to the recruitment office. The whole operation had taken less than an hour. They had said I was A-1, with a slap on the back!

The sergeant gave me a quick outline of army life, suggesting I should make my own friends and not have them pick me. "The army is made up from all sorts—don't be easily led! Now read through this paper and then we can swear you in."

The paper was mostly about swearing your loyalties to Queen and Country. "Now sign here, son, on the dotted line."

When I had signed the sergeant said, "Hold out your hand," and placed a brand new shilling into my hand. "That's the Queen's shilling, son. All we have to do now is to organise your travel documents and reporting time."

After about ten minutes, I was passed my travelling documents. "You'll report on the 8th February. You must catch the 10.15 train for London. Don't worry, son, there will be some people there to meet you. Best of luck, and I really mean that."

Later I was sitting in the Bon Bon cafe and was just taking a drink of my coffee and pondering over the morning events, when I looked up on hearing the cafe door open. Who should walk in, of all people, but Bill Hemmingway! Bill worked for the local newspaper, training to be a journalist.

"Hi Bill!" I exclaimed. "Fancy bumping into you—how's tricks?" I waited for Bill to settle down with his coffee. "Joined up, I have, Bill"—and I went on to tell him the whole story.

"Well, Alf, I think you've done the right thing. How they expect a bloke to live on ten bob a week is beyond me, but they would have got you in the end anyway."

"Going down the Victoria Hall on Saturday night, Bill?"

"Think so," he nodded. "We always seem to end up there on Saturdays."

The Victoria was the town's main dance hall. It was somewhere where we could all meet up and have a few pints and maybe check out the talent!

"What about Sunday, Alf—still going out on the bike?"

"Sure, wouldn't miss it."

Bill and me were team members of a local racing club.

"I'd like to go somewhere in the Dales, Bill," I said. "Grassington maybe, for the last time."

"Grassington would suit me Alf. Let's see what the rest of the lads think on Saturday."

"Well, there's a nice cafe there. Lets you eat your own sandwiches."

"Better be getting off, Bill." I stood up to go. "Lots of things to do before next Monday—see you on Saturday"

On Thursday I was going to go for a short spin on the bike but changed my mind. From now until next Monday I had decided to spend some quality time with my parents. I didn't know how long it would be before my first leave from the army.

On Saturday, we didn't bother with the local talent, being just content to enjoy a few pints with the lads.

Sunday arrived and we had all met at Illingworth Bend. We always met there when we were heading for the Dales. Each one of us would have a saddlebag full of sandwiches and half a crown in our back pockets. We always stopped at Skipton—that was traditional. Then on to Grassington.

We'd all gone into the tearoom and settled down with a mug of tea and our sandwiches. Derek began: "You know, lads, the bloody army has got nearly half the racing club already. Come summer and we'll be lucky to scrape a team together!"

Bill spoke in agreement. "You are bang on there, Derek. Donald Whittaker went into the army two weeks ago. David and Brierly both went into the R.A.F. three months ago, and now we are about to lose Alf."

"Yes, but they haven't got me 'til Monday. Just look out for yourselves. Wonder who will be next to receive his call up?"

It was about 6 o'clock when I arrived home. I was really hungry now. Mother always expected this and it didn't take her long to rustle up a fantastic meal.

"I had been wondering what I should be taking with me in the morning, dad."

"Nowt lad, nowt, they will only make you send it back home again. You will only need things like soap and shaving tackle. Travel light, son, that's my advice. There is a small holdall on the top of the wardrobe; that will be all you'll need, lad." He paused. "Going out tonight, son?"

"No, dad, not tonight. I'd rather spend my last night of freedom with you two—that's if I won't be in the way!" Dad smiled, and I added: "Think I'll have an early night. I'll probably need to reserve my energies for tomorrow."

Chapter Three

Monday morning arrived. I got up about seven thirty. Mother was in the kitchen.

"Dad not up yet?" I asked. "Tell you what, I'll take the old man a cup of tea up!"

"All right, but don't be long, your breakfast is almost ready."

The radio was on but there didn't seem to be much news, but that was normal. Then dad came down. Mother's voice came form the kitchen. "Breakfast is almost ready, Sidney. I hope you're feeling hungry."

"Well, you about ready, son?"

"Guess so. Packing took almost two minutes in all!"

"What bus are you catching?"

"The nine-fifteen. The train leaves at 10.15. Wouldn't want to miss it at this stage."

"No, couldn't have that lad. It would be a terrible start and that's a fact."

It was about 9.45 and I had arrived at the station. Looking back, I noticed someone walking down the road. The person seemed to be heading for the station too. As the figure drew closer, I could see he was in uniform, but there was something else about him—he looked familiar.

"Peter Wilson!" I exclaimed as he got close. Peter had been an old school chum, whom I had not seen since leaving school. "Well, I'll be blown! You're a sight for sore eyes! It's really nice to see you—been a long time. I see you're already in."

"You joining up then, Alf?"

"Yes, and it will be great to have your company down to London, Pete! See that you joined the local lot, the Duke of Wellington's Regiment."

"Yes, just been kitted out, so to speak. Now I'm off to join the battalion to begin my basic training. What about you, Alf? What lot have you joined?"

"The R.A.S.C.—was told I would be met at Kings Cross station."

He smiled and slapped me on the back. "Come on Alf, we have a train to catch!"

Standing on the platform that Monday morning, it was like the beginning of some big adventure. It had just started snowing. The first snow of winter, I thought.

Looking at my watch, it was just 10.13. "Shouldn't be long now, Pete—just a couple of minutes, that is, if the train is running on time." The train did pull in exactly on time.

"Let me give you a hand with something."

"Can you grab my kit bag, Alf?"

"Sure." It seemed to weigh a ton—it did!

We were fortunate the train wasn't overcrowded and we managed to get one of the seats with a table. With a bit of an effort I managed to get Pete's kit bag onto the rack above the seats. Peter had to strip off his backpack so that he could sit down.

"You seem to have quite a lot of kit there, Pete," I smiled. "How about a game of cards to pass a bit of time? Want to play crash, Pete?"

"Sure, why not?"

We played for about an hour and talked about our school days. It was now 11.40 and the time had passed quickly from first boarding the train at Halifax.

"Are you hungry, Alf? Let's take a stroll down to the dining carriage. I'm starving!"

After we had settled ourselves down, the waiter came ambling towards us. "What's it to be, lads—the full works? It's roast beef and Yorkshire pudding with all the trimmings."

We were soon seated with the meal in front of us and casserole dishes all over the table. There was enough food there to fill four people! It was one of those occasions when you needed to undo your top button. The meal cost us just eight shillings each and we had eaten like kings.

Once we were seated back in our carriage I asked, "Pete, what's it like then, really?"

"Well, like I said, I have only just been kitted out myself. It seemed to be done in such a hurry, lots of screaming and shouting from the N.C.O's."

"What are the N.C.O.'s, Pete?"

"Well, they are the corporals and sergeants like, a breed all on their own. They can't talk normal like you and me—they only seem to be able to scream and shout all the time. We call them the little tin gods with bird muck on their arms. You'll come to meet your own tin gods where you are going. Now that I'm joining my battalion for my proper training, that will have its fair share of them without a doubt. I suppose they will take you first to a transit camp to kit you out; then they will move you on too."

We both chattered for the rest of the journey about our experiences after leaving school. Before long the train was pulling into a station called Hendon.

"Not long now, Alf. I'd better start getting my kit off the racks."

"Let me give you a hand, Pete", I said, reaching up for his kit bag. It came down a bit easier that it went up. In fact, it nearly crowned me! "What's in it, Pete? It weighs a ton!"

"Practically half of my whole kit," he said with a big smile on his face.

After a further 15 minutes or so we arrived at Kings Cross station. Standing on the platform with all of Pete's kit around him, he asked if I could help him get it on his back. Once we had it all on him, it was just the kit bag left. "Lift it up, Alf, and plonk it on top of my backpack, across the shoulders."

When that was completed, Pete grinned. "Now just got to get to Waterloo station for my connection." He pointed to some figures and said, "I think those guys over there might be looking for you."

On the other platform there were two N.C.O.'s and they were shouting for any new enlistments. I was surprised because there must have been about thirty of us altogether. A roll call was given and then I heard my name being called: "Cartwright!" I knew I was with the right party now.

We were led through the station pretty swiftly towards where trucks were waiting.

Now the shouting and screaming started in earnest and we were bungled onto the backs of the trucks, just like cattle. The journey wasn't long, thank goodness. It was not exactly comfortable in the back of those trucks.

We eventually pulled up and were shouted off the other end. We looked all around us. First impressions were that we had been dumped into some kind of concentration camp and it was a mistake. Hell, it looked dismal! Now the N.C.O's got into full chorus and the air turned blue. It was just as if someone had put a huge key in their backs and wound them up.

It was quite dark now and the snow must have been falling constantly with huge flakes. The lads must have been freezing – I know I was.

Chapter Four

We were standing there in the freezing cold with the snow drifting down relentlessly, and separated into two groups of sixteen.

"When I shout GO," the Corporal said, "this section will double into this billet and the rest of you will double into the one over there. When I shout GO you will go in and find yourselves a bunk, deposit the rubbish you are carrying and get back outside again in two minutes. GO!"

When we entered those billet rooms, there was a row of beds down either side of the room. There was an old cast iron stove at the far end that no-one had thought to light.

Rushing back out, we couldn't help noticing a note stuck on the back of the door. It read: 'Welcome to Hell!'

Back in the ranks outside, the corporal said, "When we start off 'Quick March', you will all step off with your left foot. Let's try to keep in bloody step at least." We were marched to this large building. Inside there were two rows of tables with prepared sandwiches on them and pots of tea. We were given about ten minutes to consume them. From there we were given a quick medical.

We were all paid a ten-shilling sub and told that it wasn't for sweeties. The medical and the sub payments again only took about ten minutes. The chap standing next to me was called Burt. "What's the damned hurry? You'd think they had another bloody train to meet!"

Some of the lads started to laugh. Then we were back in the ranks again and this time we were doubled over to the quartermasters' stores and issued with sets of bedding.

After depositing the bedding in our billet rooms, it was a case of back outside in two minutes. "Now gentlemen, it's time for your kit. Let's hope we can make you lot look like ruddy soldiers." Once again we found ourselves back inside the quartermasters' stores. The kit was all laid out in one long row. We were pushed down that line; it was like a conveyor belt, as one of the lads commented later, but a lot of planning must have gone into it. The largest items, such as army greatcoats, were put across our outstretched arms, and then as you moved down the line, everything else was just plonked on top. Surprisingly, nothing seemed to fall off. Me being on the small side, I could only just make out where I was walking, placing one foot in front of the other like.

The N.C.O's were now back in full swing, shouting obscenities and cursing. Burt now had another little outburst: "Bloody little Hitlers—I'd be damned if I can move any faster!"

Once back in the billet, the corporal came in. "Remember the little sub you boys got? Well, now we are going to spend it."

Back outside, the snow seemed to be coming down even heavier. The footprints we had made earlier were almost covered.

Now we were off again—this time to some place called the N.A.A.F.I. It looked warm and inviting. "If any of you lads were thinking of getting a drink, forget it, you will be too busy tonight. We've come here to purchase cleaning materials—Blanco, Brasso, Boot polish and dusters."

Once all our purchases were completed, we fell in again outside in the snow. Because of the wind, the snow had started to drift. Hell, it was cold!

Back in the billet the corporal said, "Now lads, all I am going to show you will be completed before your bedtime. Gather around! First I will show you all how to box your blankets in the morning. This will be done every morning of your training." The corporal started folding the blankets to a certain size. The sheets were folded in the same manner exactly to the same size as the blankets. He then proceeded to stack them—blanket, sheet, blanket, sheet—to form a box. He then took the bedspread and carefully folded it around the whole structure. I recall thinking at the time that it looked quite impressive, neat, so to speak. The mattress he folded into three and placed the boxed blankets on top. "Every morning your bedding will be left like that, neat and tidy. No one will be allowed to make their beds up until 17.00 hrs. Anyone found doing so will automatically be placed on a charge. Right then, now we will concentrate on your webbing equipment. You have all been issued with a small Blanco brush like this"—which he held up for us all to see. "Now I will show you all how to apply the Blanco onto your webbing, not too thickly, and make sure you keep it even."

Then he picked something up he called a button stick. "Now this little fellow will enable you to clean your brasses without daubing your nice clean Blanco. In the morning, lads, your brasses will gleam, like everything else. Boots will be shined until you can shave in them." For the first time, someone dared to speak: "Corporal, these boots are full of pimples—how can we get a shine on them?"

"Okay, look, I'll help you out here," he conceded. "I'm not supposed to make life easy for you but just this once. You must cover each section of the boot with thick polish, and then with a very hot iron you simply burn the pimples off. But let me warn you, if you should damage your boots in the process you will be made to pay for another pair, so be careful! Battle dress and greatcoats will be pressed."

We noticed a lance corporal enter the room with an armful of brown paper and string. "One final thing, lads, strip off. Dress yourselves in your denims, which are these. You must wear your issued jungle green underpants and army socks. You have five minutes to change—get cracking!"

He then showed us how to put on our gaiters and how to fold our denim trousers over them. Now we had the task of parcelling up our civilian clothes, under the supervision of the N.C.O.'s. They were just ensuring that we did pack all our civilian clothes, including underwear and socks.

"From this moment on, it will be a chargeable offence if anyone is found wearing civilian items of clothing."

"What do you mean by a charge, corporal?"

"A charge, son, can be one or two things. Confinement to barracks or the bloody guardroom. You don't want either of those lads, believe me!"

Soon all our parcelling had been completed—all tied up and neatly addressed and finally sealed with wax. Soon both the N.C.O.'s had left us.

Fred and Andy were two teddy boys that had been called up.

They had even come wearing their Edwardian Teddy boy outfits. It was Andy who spoke. "If that bloody N.C.O. had said one more thing, I could have given him a knuckle sandwich." Everyone laughed. Burt said, "Let's get that ruddy fire lit, it's freezing in here. We might as well be warm."

It was now 19.30 hrs and Burt had got the old stove burning and we were soon beginning to feel a degree of heat coming from it. First I decided to shift all the kit off my bed and make it up. Now I was going to give myself five minutes to relax. Stretching myself out on the bed, my thought took me back over the day. Yes, it had certainly been an adventure. Then my thoughts turned to home and mother and father. If only they could have seen me now! Father would probably be smoking that old pipe of his. He never told me what to expect—he probably didn't want to put me off! Then I thought of my cycling friends and that last ride out to Grassington in the Dales.

But now I was back in the present, looking around and all I could see was kit everywhere.

The guy in the next bunk was called Stanley Crawford and he was smaller than me. I was just five foot four in my stocking feet. Stan must have only been about five foot. We seemed to hit it off from the start. I found out that Stan came from Wigan. Once we had teamed up it didn't take us long to sort our kit out. In fact, everyone helped each other that night. If someone got stuck, someone would jump up and help out.

Stan and I started on our webbing equipment first. By 22.30 hrs I could have murdered for a cup of tea. One of the lads shouted: "Oh bloody hell!" He was standing in the middle of the barrack room with one of his boots in his hand. All we could see was that the boots he was holding were just falling apart. In fact, we all saw the boot cap fall off and drop to the floor. He must have ironed over the stitching. Everyone just roared and someone shouted: "The first casualty of 'C' block!"

Burt shouted: "How about some music lads?" Then he extracted a small radio from its hiding place.

"How the hell did you manage that?"

"Hid it inside my mattress, like, when we first came in here. I knew that those bastards would have confiscated it if they had found it. In the future it will be much easier to hide it with all this kit."

Some of the lads were now sitting around the stove, which was now glowing. They were busy trying to get some sort of shine on their boots. It was getting late and soon most of the lads were stretched out on their beds. Some were enjoying a cigarette and listening to the music drifting across the room from Burt's radio.

No doubt some would be thinking of home, wives, girlfriends. Most of us had never been away from home before. Our journey had only started that morning—it had been a long day. Normality seemed to be something we had all lost since arriving at this camp. Stan and I finished our webbing equipment. It seemed okay to us but I'll bet the N.C.O.'s will pull it to pieces in the morning. We had also been successful in burning the pimples off our boots, without them falling apart. Now we were both sitting around that old stove buffing our boots. It was the first time I had been warm since we had arrived. All the boys were chatting away, some cursing, some laughing.

The music was still drifting across the room. The music seemed to be bringing some form of normality back to us all. Most of the lads must have been pretty tired by this time. Stan and I certainly were.

The time was drawing close to midnight now. We hadn't stopped since arriving there. We all felt we had been there forever. What a bloody day! Some shouted: "Let's all call it a day and turn in—what isn't completed, isn't completed. Suppose they will have a go at all of us in the morning anyway. Can't put us all on a bloody charge, can they? Does anyone know what time the bloody Gestapo will be coming around in the morning?"

No one knew, but no doubt they would make their presence known.

We all decided to get some sleep and forget everything till morning. In the darkness my thoughts drifted to home and friends and then I must have dropped off.

Chapter Five

We were awakened to the sound of clattering dustbin lids. The N.C.O.'s were back. They were obviously creating as much noise as humanly possible by beating the dustbin lids with drill sticks. The verbal abuse soon followed. "Come on, you bloody lot, out of bed! The time is 07.00 hrs. Breakfast is 07.30 hrs. I'm sure that even you lot will be able to find the cookhouse. At 08.00 hrs you will all be out on parade wearing your battle dress and greatcoats." Then they disappeared again. One chap quietly spoke: "Do they have to bang those bloody dustbin lids and create such a goddamn noise? Could give us sensitive ones a heart attack."

Stan laughed. "Better get used to it, Bob. I've a feeling they've started as they mean to go on."

The cookhouse was warm and welcoming. As we entered

we could smell the aroma of bacon and sausage. We all joined the queue. The food was fantastic and as much bread and butter as one could eat. Stan said, "I wonder what they are feeding us up for?" But then breakfast was good and we weren't going to complain.

The time seemed to fly and we were soon standing outside again on parade. Our blankets had been boxed and the old stove had been cleaned and re-set.

We were standing in about six inches of snow and it was still coming down steadily. The N.C.O.'s now reappeared. "We've looked inside the billets and they are bloody awful! Your boxed blankets are not good enough, the ablutions haven't been touched, the floors have not been swept let alone polished, and there is bloody dust everywhere! Standards will improve! If not, we will start to jump all over you. Privileges will be stopped.

"Now the lance corporal will come around and give you all a slip of paper. On the paper you will find a number—your own personal army number. Remember it! This afternoon your number will be stencilled onto your kit bag along with your rank and name.

"We are going to march onto the parade ground. The Commanding officer always likes to have a word with all new recruits and introduce himself, like. To start with from the 'at ease' position, lift the right leg up waist belt high and drive it sharply alongside your left foot. Now you are 'standing to attention'. To go back to 'at ease', the right leg will again be lifted waist high and again driven down two feet away from your left foot."

We practised this a few times and the N.C.O. stopped swearing. We must have been getting the hang of it. The right and left turns were executed by pivoting on the balls of the feet to a ninety-degree angle and the rear leg brought up waist belt high and again driven alongside the other foot. The corporal demonstrated each move. "That's how I want you lot to do it!"

We now set off for the parade ground. It had started snowing heavily again. I did remember how grateful we were to have been wearing those greatcoats. It was freezing. When we halted it was a shambles. We were quickly told to get our dressing again and stand still until the Major arrived. The Major talked at length, telling us that it would get much tougher when we started our proper training a week on Monday.

On leaving the parade ground, the corporal said we would be taken to the drill sheds for more drill before our NAAFI break. NAAFI break? That sounded like a privilege, that did! He made us drill for about an hour, wanting us to swing our arms shoulder high. He went through the roof if we didn't. The second time the corporal shouted "Halt" we still hadn't been shown yet. I actually felt sorry for him; we were too close to the wall. We all ended up piling into one another, legs and bodies all over the place. It gave us a bit of a laugh but the corporal was fuming. "Watch him Stan; he might burst a bloody blood vessel if we're lucky!"

We were taken to the NAAFI. It was like a huge cafe. Two young girls were serving. That was a treat in its own right for the lads! One was a redhead, about five three, slim and attractive. The other was about the same height but brunette and nicely proportioned. From talking to Stan the other night I knew his preferences was for redheads.

"Put your eyes back, Stan, she's probably spoken for!"

Anyway, the way I saw it, the girls would be given chat up lines every day. Plus, we were only there for a couple of weeks ourselves.

"Can't stop a guy from looking, Alf. She's a bit of a dazzler, you've got to admit!"

Stan and I got a couple of sausage rolls and a pot of tea.

10.30 hrs and we were back out in the snow and marching back down to the bleeding drill sheds. Same as before, except this time the corporal instilled into us the way to halt correctly and seemed amazed how quickly we got the hang of it. At least we were doing something right! Burt burst out: "Haven't you realised yet, lads, that it doesn't matter how we fair, they will find fault, just for the goddamn hell of it! That's why they are enjoying themselves so bloody much!"

12.00 hrs, and dinnertime. Again the food was faultless. We got a whole hour for dinner and then strolled back down to the NAAFI for twenty minutes or so. For Stan, I think it was just the scenery, but for me it was better than the billet room. We couldn't make our beds just to lie on them. Blankets had to be kept boxed till after tea, plus we couldn't light the ruddy stove either and it was freezing. But here in the NAAFI it was warm, light, and of course the scenery wasn't bad either.

13.00 hrs we were back on parade. The N.C.O.'s started to inspect us walking down each line, along the front and then down the back.

"If I had to find fault with one of you," said the corporal, "we would be all bloody day. When I say 'Go', get back into the billets and stand by your beds—'GO!'"

The N.C.O.'s entered, the lance corporal carrying a complete stencil kit. "I really hope that none of you lot has lost his army number from this morning. It would give me great delight to make out some 252's charge sheets."

It must have taken a couple of hours to finish off all the stencilling. Someone said, "What now, Corp?" The corporal turned, stared at him. "Stand to attention whenever you talk to me and that goes for all of you lot! My rank is corporal, not corp! Remember that and we might get on. These stripes on my arm are not bird muck and I damn well had to earn them!"

My mind went back to Kings Cross station, to when my school chum had said, "You will find your own tin gods with bird muck, Alf." So the corporal kept rabbiting on: "...and that goes for all the N.C.O.'s; you will stand to attention whenever you speak to them. In other words, lads, when we say Shit, you will jump on the shovel!"

The lance corporal's voice droned on: "Now we have much to cover before your tea." He produced what was referred to as a bumper. A bumper was a long pole with a heavy weight on one end. The pole was attached by a pivot into the centre of the weight. The idea was to swing the thing backwards and forwards across the floor. Polish was liberally spread on the floor and the bumper acted as a huge polisher. To finish off, dusters were tied around the head of the bumper for a final polish. The action of the working bumper had been carefully displayed by the lance corporal.

"Floors will gleam, boys, gleam! It is Tuesday today; now, on Thursday it will be the old man's inspection. The Major, that is. Tomorrow you will all be shown how to lay out your kit on your beds. I am expecting a good standard from you lot. Don't disappoint me or, like I said earlier, privileges will be stopped—especially if I get it in the neck from the Major. Tomorrow you will be taught how to salute correctly. Plus weapons drill." He gave a grim smile. "Now don't get excited, lads—ammunition will not be issued, so if you guys had any ideas about me, forget it!" That brought a bit of a titter from the lads at the back. "Tomorrow we will be a little bit better organised."

The corporal picked out two of the lads and allotted them the task of cleaning out the ablutions every morning. Another man was given the task of looking after the fire buckets, checking the sand and water levels each day, and yet another lad was responsible for cleaning and re-setting the stove each day. "The rest of you lot will all muck in and sweep and polish around their beds. That is, around the beds of those men who have been allocated jobs by me. You will all help each other with your kit layouts in the morning. Now I'll let you guys get on with the floor. Remember, lads—glass, just like glass! Also, before I go, don't forget the buffing of your boots, brasses and press those uniforms. A hot iron and brown paper does help." And then he disappeared.

One of the lads chirped up: "Well, look at it this way, at least we will have a better chance of getting it right in the morning—a better chance than yesterday."

Pete retorted: "15.30 hrs, an hour and half to tea, then it's down to the NAAFI for a pint. Let's gets cracking lads, let's get on top of this floor now!"

About 20.00 hrs Stan and I wandered down to the NAAFI. Walking down, Stan said, "I wish we were able to get a pint." Entering the NAAFI we looked around; didn't seem to be many lads in. The two young girls weren't there, much to Stan's disappointment. There were in their place, two middle-aged women serving behind the counter.

"Just a mo, Stan," I said, "I think there's another room around the back."

"Let's investigate, Alf," Stan suggested.

We walked through into another room and there was a bar, tables and chairs and in the far corner a billiard table. On the other side of the room two lads were playing darts.

"This do you, Stan?"

"Bloody fantastic, Alf, I'll get us a couple of pints!"—and we settled down.

"Now this is more like it." After a couple of hours we wandered back to the billet.

Wednesday was more drill till dinnertime, but we did have our NAAFI break again.

After dinner we were given about half a dozen sheets of paper with the kit layout on, which we needed for the old man's kit inspection in the morning. Then back to buffing our boots and desperately trying to get some shine on our brasses. The floor seemed to have a good shine on it now; wouldn't take much buffing in the morning.

Thursday the kit inspection went well. The major said that considering we had only been in the army for a few days, we had done well. "Bloody good show, well done!"

It was refreshing coming from the major. Not what the N.C.O.'s had been saying before he arrived. He just about pulled everything to bits. The day followed in much the same way as the previous days—drill and more drill, bull and more bull.

Friday arrived and we got our pay. I was sorry because most of the lads were National Service and the money they got paid was like survival money. Saturday and Sunday was our time. Time to write letters home and time to relax. But come Monday and it was back to the square bashing in the drill sheds. It was like that all week, similar to the first week really. Friday seemed to come around quickly and we were paid again.

The nice surprise was that we were going to be allowed out of the barracks for the first time. We would have to pass through the guardroom to get out, so battle dresses would have to be pressed.

After tea that night, everybody was busy pressing uniforms and excited. It was like not seeing civilization for two whole weeks. We found ourselves walking towards the guardroom—it was just 17.00 hrs. The guard commander looked us over. "Turn around lads—you'll do. Now don't let's get into any fights tonight. Keep your noses clean."

Once we were clear of the guardroom, Stan shouted: "Freedom at last!" We didn't really know where we were, apart from being just on the outskirts of London.

We found a nice little pub and went in. Inside we noticed one or two of our lads already in, playing darts. After I had bought Stan and myself a pint we found ourselves some seats.

"Now Stan, the drinks are on me tonight, no arguing."

"But Alf…"

"No buts Stan; look, you're only on National Service pay, plus we're celebrating." Looking around the room, I spotted them. "Don't look now, Stan, but you know the two crackers from the NAAFI? Well, they're sat over there!"

"Bloody Hell, Alf, let's see if we can buy them a drink!"

We both stood up and walked over to them. "Can we join you girls?"

"Why not?" stated the redhead and grinned.

"What would you girls like to drink?"

"We'll both have half a glass of best bitter lads, and thanks."

"Come on, Stan, let's get these lovely girls a drink."

At the bar, Stan said, "Bloody hell, Alf, I think we've cracked it!"

Rejoining the girls, I said, "Look, my name is Alf, and my friend here is called Stan."

"Nice to meet you boys and thanks for the drinks," said the redhead. "I'm called Peggy and my friend's name is Sue."

"You must be joking! Isn't there a song call that—Peggy

Sue?"

Sue smiled. "Look lads, everyone says that, but honestly, that's our names"—and we all laughed. Stan sat next to Peggy and I sat with Sue. We just seemed to talk and talk as if we'd known each other for ages.

Sue said: "Where are you and Stan going tomorrow?"

"Yeovil and Summerset. We'll be doing our driver training there."

Sue exclaimed, "What a coincidence! Me and Peggy come from around there, a small place called Mattock. We were both sent to work here when we joined the NAAFI."

The girls wouldn't let us pay for any more drinks that night, but thanked us for the first drink. They said they knew what the army paid us, a pittance.

The girls had quarters in the barracks so we were all able to walk back together.

"Come on girls, how about a good night kiss?"

We kissed and we all wished each other the best. "Good night Peggy, good night Sue."

I thought Stan would be having pleasant dreams that night!

Chapter Six

Saturday morning, and we had all handed our bedding in by 08.00 hrs. It hadn't snowed overnight and the sky was clear blue and there was a nip in the air. The snow had a thin layer of ice over it: when you walked in it you could feel it crunch under your boots.

Back inside the billets, the lads where busy packing their kit. The corporal had advised us to pack as much as we could squeeze into our kit bags. "We can't go to the training camp with paper carrier bags, can we now?"

The sarcastic little sod, I thought!

The difficulty we found was in our webbing equipment, which strap went where and then adjusting it. We couldn't have done all this on our own; we all had to help each other.

The corporal's name was Armstrong. No one used his name;

the boys had made up their own names for him. However, he had told us to be out on parade in full kit, carrying out kit bags by 10.00 hrs.

It was fine but ruddy cold! We were marched to a small vehicle park to the right of the guardroom. When we arrived there, two army trucks were waiting for us. Probably the very same two that had brought us there.

"Quickly lads, scramble onto the trucks." We were like sardines, our equipment took up so much room.

We had to stand up in the back of the trucks because of our kit. Burt said, "Here's for a bumpy ride, lads!" The trucks pulled off and we had to hang onto each other to stop falling over. It took about twenty minutes from the camp to the train station.

We piled out and were quickly led onto the platform to await our train. They'd told us that the train would take us to Yeovil where we would be met. Carriages had been reserved for us on our journey.

Once on the train we were able to take our packs off and settle down. Some of the lads lit cigarettes and smoked. The journey took about two and a half hours and it was nice just to relax. We had some idea now what the welcoming party would be like. The train pulled in at Yeovil station and we started tumbling out.

The N.C.O.'s that were there started screaming at us as we struggled to get our packs back on. Once more we were hurriedly put on to waiting trucks. Again the journey in the trucks took about twenty minutes. Stan and I were standing near the back of the truck and we could see out. Passing through Yeovil town, it didn't seem such a bad place. We estimated that the camp was only about a mile from the town.

Arriving at our new camp, the N.C.O.'s were shouting for us

to get off the trucks and form three ranks. They marched us to our new billets, which they called spider huts, possibly because of how they had been designed.

They were quite large and all thirty-two of us could easily be accommodated in one spider hut. "When I shout 'Go', you lot get inside, dump your kit and get back out here in two minutes—G O!"

Other N.C.O.'s followed us in and delegated where each one of us would sleep. Stan and I managed to get in the same room. There seemed to be N.C.O.'s everywhere, all screaming at the same time.

"Come on you horrible lot, get outside now!" We were then taken and issued with the old bedding again and quickly doubled back to the spider hut. We had to dump the bedding and be back outside again in two minutes. Stan whispered to me: "Couldn't they make it three bloody minutes?"

Once we were back in three ranks, the corporal addressed us: "My name is Corporal Briggs and don't forget it. When you wish to speak to me, or any of my N.C.O.'s, you will jump to attention. This will be your home now for the next ten weeks and you will all be referred to as 'C' platoon. Now 'C' platoon, 'C' platoon, Shun! Turn to your right in three, right turn. Stand still, you horrible misfits, stand still! You will now be given a guided tour. Shown around the camp, all the places of interest."

They marched us off. We were halted whenever the corporal wanted to point something out—cookhouse, the M.T. sheds, the NAAFI and finally the gym. "You lads will be spending a lot of time in there—intend to get you sloppy lot fit. The time is now 14.00 hrs and you will have missed dinner so you will be allowed thirty minutes to visit the NAAFI, then make your way back to the spider and start sorting your kit out. Make the most of today lads—there will be no more free meal tickets after today."

The NAAFI was much larger than at the last camp and the girls were not as pretty.

"Could eat a horse, Stan!"

"Me too," replied Stan with feeling.

Later, back in the spider, we were all relaxing. We had sorted our kit out. Most of the lads were sitting on their beds bulling their best boots. A lance corporal had been around earlier and had shown us how our webbing equipment had to be laid out on the tops of our lockers.

I looked at Stan. "Hi Stan, have you seen Peter Griffith's boots? They're like glass!"

"Bloody hell, Alf, let's wander down and ask him if he can show us."

"Hi Pete, we were noticing your boots and what a great shine you're getting. How about showing me and Stan?"

"It will cost you a pint, lads. All you do, Alf, is spit onto the toe cap, just a bit mind, and then put your finger through the duster and apply some polish. Now rub the polish in, in little circles. It's a bit tedious but the idea is to build up the polish. The more you build it up, the greater the shine."

"Great, let's try it, Stan!"

We got to work on our own boots and we soon started to get the same results.

Someone shouted: "Tea time, lads!"—and we all started heading towards the cookhouse. The cookhouse was an enormous size and, like other places, the food was plentiful.

About 19.00 hrs, I looked across at Pete in the corner. "Come on Pete, let's get you that pint!"—and we all wandered up to the NAAFI.

"How's the boots coming on?"

"Great, we're beginning to get them like yours now!"

The only beverages they sold in the NAAFI besides tea and coffee was this stuff called cider. Stan and I thought it was just pop, so we had a few pints. It wasn't until we got outside that it hit us. Pete laughed: "Got quite a kick, that cider, hasn't it, lads! I must admit I feel a bit tipsy myself."

"What time is reveille in the morning?" Stan asked. Someone mentioned 06.00 hrs. "Hell, that's early, isn't it? Think I'll start keeping a calendar like, to mark off these ten weeks we have to stay in this hell-hole," and added, "Day by day!"

Tuesday morning, we were awakened by lots of screaming and shouting, minus the dustbin lid treatment, for which we were all grateful. "You will stand by your beds by 6.45 hrs when billets will be inspected. We demand high standards!"

Everyone was busy boxing blankets, bumping the floors and some of us got stuck into the ablutions. They came back at exactly 06.45 hrs. They ripped us to pieces, making our efforts seem like nothing. "You are all going to have to do much better than this! You will all go now for your breakfast and be back on parade by 07.45 hrs."

"Hell, Alf, I know what I'm going to do," Stan said. "I'm going to press my battle dress the night before and lay my kit out, ready to jump into it. It would give us more time in the morning."

"Been thinking on the same lines, Stan."

We'd eaten breakfast and were now standing in three ranks again outside. The N.C.O.'s arrived. One of them shouted, "Stand still," and they began inspecting us, finding fault with each one of us. They got to Stan and me and screamed: "Why have you two not shaved this morning?"

"But we don't shave, corporal—never have," I replied defensively.

"You have bum fluff on your faces! It will be shaved off in the morning. If you haven't got a razor, I suggest you both buy one! Now all of you need a haircut before we do anything else!"

The corporal was overseeing our haircuts, instructing the barbers to cut it close. We felt as if we had been almost scalped.

We were marched out onto the parade ground, where a huge sergeant was waiting for us. "My name is sergeant Hirst and I hate everybody, especially you lot! It's my job to whip you all into shape and make soldiers out of you all." We were brought to attention. "Move to the right in three's, right turn, quick march! Now dig you heels in, dig them in! Let me hear them! Swing your bloody arms shoulder high, damn you, get them up! Press your thumbs down on your hands and keep these arms straight. Impress me! That man there, if you don't swing your bloody arms shoulder high, I will snap it off and hit you with the soggy end!"

It wasn't that the air was blue; he came out with things our innocent ears weren't used to. It was hard not to laugh but we knew that if we did, he would jump all over us. Finally we stopped and were handed over again to the corporal. The corporal smirked: "Bet you enjoyed that, lads!"—and we were marches off to the NAAFI.

After NAAFI break, we were marched back to our billets. When the corporal halted us he said, "When I say, go, go inside and I want you back outside in two minutes in PE kit!" Everyone dashed inside and hurriedly changed. "Come on, you lot, move yourselves!" Once outside the corporal said, "Not fast enough! You lot haven't grasped the message yet. When I say two minutes, I bloody well mean *two minutes*, not three!"

Now we were doubling to the Gym and had a vigorous hour's training. The ropes got a couple of the lads—they just couldn't climb them. The PE instructor was doing his nut and just kept on at them.

After dinner, it was a repeat performance of what we had done in the morning. Drill followed the gym. After tea, Burt said, "What a bloody day, lads. Wonder what they've got lined up for us tomorrow!"

Pete said, "Couldn't care less, right at this minute, Burt. Just going to do my kit and then off to the NAAFI—try to forget it all for awhile, that's my advice."

Stan and I didn't go out that night—watching our money, you might say. It was still a few days off payday and we didn't want to run out.

There were only a few of us that stayed in. Opposite Pete's bed was a chap called Bill Whitely—a quiet lad who didn't seem to mix a lot. There was something about Bill, a kind of sadness, but most of the lads spoke to him in a friendly manner.

It was Friday morning on the parade ground. The sergeant had been demonstrating turnings on the march and during practice, the sergeant screamed: "Right turn!" Bill turned left and it threw everyone out.

The sergeant went mad. "Stand still, you horrible lot!" Then he went straight to Bill. "Are you bloody deaf, soldier?"

Bill looked at the sergeant and spoke very quietly. "Look, sergeant, I can't hear you when you are on my right-hand side. Perforated ear drum, sergeant."

This fair knocked the wind out of the sergeant's sails. "Look lad, you can get out of the army with that."

"But sergeant, I don't want to be out of the army."

"From now on then, son, I'll try to be aware of that for you." It was the first time we had seen the human side to sergeant Hirst.

We drew our pay that afternoon and that evening Stan and I talked. "Look Stan, I think I will go over and have a word with Bill over there, see if he will join us when we go to the NAAFI."

"Okay, Alf, though I doubt it. But you can try."

I strolled over and sat on the edge of Bill's bed. "Some of the lads were wondering why you don't want to get out, Bill?"

"It's simple really. I if tell you something, can we keep it between you and me? Don't want it broadcasted, really. About three months ago both my parents were killed outright in a car accident. Couldn't see myself wandering about in that big house, it would have driven me nuts, so I joined up."

"I'm really sorry, Bill, I shouldn't have asked."

"Its okay, Alf, thank you for showing concern."

"Look, Bill, Stan and I wondered if you would join us up the NAAFI."

"Why not, Alf, I'd be glad of the company."

"Look Bill, we are your family now—the whole ruddy lot of us."

Up at the NAAFI we chatted about all sorts of things, but what everyone wanted to know was when the driving instruction would start. Bill said, "Oh I know, after next week, week this Monday, like."

"Great!" exclaimed Stan. "Can't wait."

The next week flew by; it was like the first week except for a six-mile route march on Wednesday.

Chapter Seven

The time was just 16.45 hrs. We had just been brought back to the spider and the corporal had just shouted the order for dismissal. I remember feeling, well that's it now, weekend once again and on Monday, we will start our driving. Well, I thought, that was it and then I heard Stan stop to attention. Stan was addressing the lance corporal:

"Corporal, here you are"—and Stan offered the N.C.O. a new sixpence.

"What's that for, lad?"

"So you can take a slow boat to China."

The corporal looked at Stan and said, "Nice one, report to the cookhouse after your tea, Crawford—cookhouse fatigues."

I said, "That's a bit unfair, Corporal."

He looked at me and said, "You can join him then, Cartwright."

It reminded me of Stan and Oliver Hardy from the films. I just looked at Stan and said, "Another fine mess, Stanley."

We reported to the cookhouse at 18.00 hrs and were led into the back of the cookhouse, facing two sinks. They resembled two huge vats and there seemed to be hundreds of plates there. Stan looked at me and said, "Bloody Hell, Alf." The plates were greasy and guess what—the water was cold. It must have been 23.00 hrs when we finally got out of there.

In the morning at breakfast, we both agreed that we wouldn't want to do those cookhouse fatigues again in a hurry. Then Stan said, "It was bloody worth it all, Alf, just to see the corporal's face when I told him what to do with the sixpence!"

We carried on eating and then the orderly officer came by. "You boys going to eat all that bread?"

Stan and I had about eight slices in front of us. "Yes sir."

"Very well, lads, that's fine. We don't want to waste food—carry on."

After the meal we went back down to the spider. "Lets get everything sorted out, shipshape for Monday, then the rest of the weekend is ours."

"Tell you what, fancy having a walk into Yeovil after dinner? We haven't been out of this place in almost two weeks."

So after dinner, we got ourselves ready for Yeovil but we needed to book out of the guardroom. Three times we reported and three times we were sent back, being told we were not good enough. "He's having a damned laugh, Alf, come on." We searched the perimeter fence, found a gap and climbed through.

It took us only twenty minutes to walk into Yeovil. I suppose it was just like any other small town.

We looked around all the shops first and then found ourselves a nice cafe and had ourselves a cuppa. We then checked out the local dance hall.

"Back here tonight eh, Stan?"

"Why not—and we can check out the local talent at the same time!"

We got back to the camp about 16.00 hrs and quietly sneaked back through the wire.

"We'll be going out the same way tonight, Alf, sod the ruddy guardroom."

Back in the billet, we soon learnt that a few of the lads had the same idea as us and used the break in the perimeter fence.

Pete and Burt had brought back into the camp some sheets of hardboard and a small saw and were busy cutting it up. Stan and I were just lying on our beds and watching what they were doing. They carefully measured and cut each piece and then proceeded placing them into their webbing equipment. Large and small packs and even their bullet pouches, boxing them off like, giving them a nice square off look. Stan and I got up and walked across to their beds.

"Looking good, Pete, but how the hell did you get them past the guardroom?"

"Don't ask!" Pete exclaimed.

Burt said, "One of us got through the wire and the other hurled them over the top. Great, eh! Look, Alf, there's plenty left over, enough for you and Stan to box yours off."

"Thanks Pete, it's good of you both."

It was now time for tea; at least we wouldn't go hungry. "Wonder who is doing the washing up tonight, Stan?"

"Well, it isn't us Alf; we're out on the town."

About 19.00 hrs we all started filtering out of the spider. We had decided to leave a two-minute interval. Not a good idea if all thirty of us headed for the wire at once—someone might have noticed, like! We all met up on the road and headed for Yeovil.

The dance hall was quite big. In the centre of the ceiling there was one of those glistening balls, turning and reflecting rays of light around the room. The band had just struck up and started playing a quick step.

There was always a full live band playing in the local dance halls. On the night, all the rockers were in full swing. Fred and Andy, the two ex-Teds, we're over there bopping away and swinging two girls around.

Stan and I, we stood there scanning the room. Stan spotted two girls dancing together.

"How about those two, Alf—have we to split them, eh?"

"Okay, come on!"

"Excuse me," we both said in unison and we both grabbed one each.

We seemed to hit it off from the start. About 22.00 hrs I suggested we leave and have a quiet drink. Later we walked the girls to their bus stop, after arranging to meet them the day after. We all arranged to see a film at the local cinema.

When we finally did get back to camp, much of the camp seemed to be in darkness. We quietly made our way back to the spider, and made it undetected. We slept until 08.00 hrs in the morning and then wandered up to the cookhouse for breakfast.

Later, lying on our beds in the billet room, we listened to the lads bantering on about their exploits the previous evening.

We were all only young lads in those days and young men

have a tendency to romance a little bit. I know that we said we would relax for the rest of the weekend but we found ourselves rebalancing our webbing and skimming our brasses again. Finally, we gave our boots an extra polish.

However, we did then crash out. We were just lying on our beds and listening to Burt's radio. I decided to take advantage of the free time and write home again. I let my parents have my new address. It would be great to receive a letter from home.

About 18.45 hrs we set off once more for Yeovil and to meet up again with the two young girls from last night.

The film was called 'Gone with the Wind'. Not my or Stan's cup of tea, but the girls seemed to really enjoy it.

Afterwards, we walked them both back to their bus and kissed them goodnight. We hadn't made any firm arrangements to meet up with them again the following week.

Chapter Eight

It was the 23rd March. Spring had arrived, the long hard winter seemed to be behind us, and the sun was shining.

We were standing outside the spider in three ranks. The N.C.O.'s had stopped balling at us and we were now being inspected. It was the usual banter:

"Am I hurting you, son?"

"No corporal."

"Well, I bloody well ought to be—I'm standing on your hair! Get it cut!"

Corporal Briggs addressed us. "You will be starting your driver training this morning, The next two weeks you will be driving in the mornings from 08.00 hrs to 12.00 hrs. It will then be square-bashing in the afternoons, plus whatever else we can think up for you. The second fortnight will be reversed with drill and weapons in the morning, followed again by driving in the afternoons."

We were marched to the vehicle park. "Swing your bloody shoulder high and let me hear you driving your ruddy heels in!"

The vehicle park was square and the trucks were lined up on three sides. "When you hear your name called out, you will snap to attention. You will then be allocated a truck and your new driving instructor. Now stand still!"

My name was called eventually and I snapped to attention. The truck I was allocated was no. 27 and the instructor's name was Mr Stansfield, ex-army captain. I think that all the instructors were civilians but ex-army personnel. All or most, no doubt, from the last war.

When I climbed into that cab, it felt huge and a bit daunting. The instructor asked me, "Have you ever ridden a cycle son?"

"Yes sir."

"And did it have gears?"

"Yes sir."

"Well, the gears on your cycle enabled you to go up hills easier. Well, the gears on this truck act in the same way. Now this is a gear lever." He went through all the basics and we finally set off.

The instructor drove until we had filled up with petrol and got outside the camp. Progress was slow to start with, but I found myself rather enjoying myself.

About 10.00 hrs, the instructor indicated for me to turn off and pull over. We were outside a cafe. The cafe was called the Rod House Café. It was at Blythe on the Worksop Road, near Bedford. I still remember walking into that cafe and ordering a Mr. Kipling tart and a pot of tea.

Those four hours seemed to fly that first morning. You know what they say about time, when you are enjoying yourself. Well, it certainly flew that morning!

After dinner, we were marched to the armoury and withdrew our rifles for arms drill on the square. It's funny but you can almost guarantee that some poor sod will drop his rifle. Today wasn't an exception. It went with a right clatter. Again, the sergeant was fuming. I could have sworn I saw steam coming from his nostrils!

After tea, back in the billet, all the lads were recalling their experiences of the day.

The following three weeks flew by, possibly because the driver training broke up the square bashing. Towards the end of the third week, some of the lads had successfully passed their test. Poor Dell had failed his test four times. So the chief instructor took Dell out but couldn't find fault with his driving. "Why do you think you are failing so much, son?"

"It's my instructor sir, always shouting and making me nervous like."

Dell was given another instructor and then went on to pass his test the very next time.

April 17th was the date I finally passed my test. In fact, Stan passed his test on the very same day—Stan in the morning and me in the afternoon, It was the day before my 18th birthday so it was an excuse to celebrate the following weekend.

Easter was rapidly approaching and a rumour had been circulating round that we might be sent home on leave. On that next Monday morning on the parade ground, the sergeant announced it. "Leave for you lads, from Thursday, with the exception of six men from 'C' platoon. These men will be held back for guard duties over the holiday."

He then started reading out loud from the list he was holding: "Crawford, Cartwright, Griffiths…"

"I bloody *knew* it, Stan, that my name and your name would be at the top of the list!" It felt just like a black cloud was coming over us. Hell, we were really looking forward to going home.

The guard duties were over twenty four hour periods. Twenty-four on and twenty-four off. Stan and I were on the first guard. Guard mounting consisted of the guard, the guard commander was a full corporal. His second in command was a lance corporal, the orderly sergeant and the orderly officer.

Guard mounting was inspected by the orderly officer and then we were dispersed into the guardroom. Stan and I were on the first watch with two other drivers. The guard consisted of twelve of us working on two hours on and four hours off around the clock.

Four of us that were on guard duty first were then positioned around the camp. I found myself patrolling the perimeter wire. As I was walking around my thoughts were of home, thinking of all the luck, when I could have been on my way home. Well, you win some and you lose some, I thought.

When the guard was changed over, I found it difficult to switch off and sleep over the next four hours. I suppose my mind was overactive.

Our first stint on guard duty ended at 18.00 hrs the following day. This meant that we were off duty for the next twenty-four hours until 18.00 hrs the following day. After a late tea, we decided we would slip into Yeovil and spend some quality time, checking out one or two local pubs.

The following morning we had both decided to skip breakfast and catch up on some well-deserved sleep.

We had, I suppose, a pretty lazy day, except for checking out our kit, i.e. pressing our uniforms and shining our boots and brasses, for the coming guard mounting at 18.00 hrs that day.

It also meant we had only one more twenty-four hour guard to complete and we would have done our first stint over the Easter break. At least those few days had been peaceful without the N.C.O.'s screaming at us at every turn.

We mounted guard at 18.00 hrs again and it was the usual two on and four off. Stan and I did manage to get some shuteye on our four hours off, this time. After our final stint on guard duty it was Sunday evening. We didn't really know if the lads would be back that evening or tomorrow, Monday.

When the lads did eventually arrive back, we started the final week in the driving school. The weather was still getting warmer.

Stan said, "How many of the lads have to pass their test yet, Alf?"

"Don't know, Stan, but it's not many; probably five or six, should all be passed before the end of the week." And they did all eventually pass.

The last two weeks of training were spent rehearsing the passing out parade, with the exception of a route march on each Wednesday.

The drill sergeant, sergeant Hirst, was fine-tuning us. Everything we did had to be just right. One morning he addressed us: "Inside the butts of your lea Enfield rifle there is a small plate were your pull through is housed. Take the pull through out and replace it with a penny. Tomorrow morning each of you will have a penny placed in the butt of your rifles."

The day after, when we went on parade, all armed with pennies, the drill sergeant went through ordering and sloping arms and finally presenting arms.

"Now I want you all to really crack those rifles! Let me hear those pennies rattle. It's just a bit of bull, lads, but on the final day it will give your passing out parade that little extra polish."

The final day arrived and we marched onto the parade ground. The sergeant shouted: "Parade, parade, parade, halt!" Some of the lad's families had travelled down to watch their sons pass out. Unfortunately for Stan and me, the distance was too far.

Standing on the parade ground that Saturday morning with the sun on our backs, we stood there gleaming, all bullied up to the eyebrows.

We had a full military band. The band struck up and the sergeant screamed, "Quick march!" The sergeant whispered, "Bags of swank, lads!"

We felt like a million dollars on that morning and I guess just a little proud as we dug our heels in and swung our arms shoulder high, everyone in perfect lines.

After the parade was over, the sergeant again addressed us: "Well done, lads, you have done everybody proud. Tomorrow is yours—you can start packing your kit. You are going home on Monday on embarkation leave. On Monday morning you will be given your travel warrants and instructions on how and where to report afterwards. You will also be told where you are being posted. When I give the order 'dismiss', the one's whose parents are here, you may join them—Dismiss!"

Chapter Nine

It was now the 11th May 1956. After breakfast we were standing in three ranks, outside the spider in full service marching order. The time was exactly 09.00 hrs.

We were marched onto the parade ground where two trucks were waiting. We scrambled onto the trucks. When the engines started up, I said, "Well, we're on our way now, Stan, on our way home; can't believe the training is all over!"

"I'm glad we are leaving and not just arriving, eh, Alf!"

Out of the thirty-two of us, twenty-five of us were being posted to Germany. Plus, we had been given three weeks' embarkation leave.

We were soon all standing on the platform at Yeovil station, waiting for the train to whisk us off to London. The journey took just under two and half hours and the train pulled into Waterloo Station. Both Stan and I needed to get to Kings Cross station so we set off down the subway.

At Kings Cross, Stan needed to catch the 11.45 hrs to Manchester. My train was due to pull out at 11.57 hrs. We both had about 30 minutes to wait so we decided on a cup of 'rosie lee'.

My train pulled in—it was the Flying Scotsman. Great, I'd heard someone remark that this beauty travelled like the wind!

In the middle of the train, one carriage had been made into a bar. Getting myself a drink, I stood and looked out of the window for a while. The train did seem to be motoring a bit. Probably doing about 80 miles per hour. Settling in one of the carriages, I must have dozed off. Awakened by a jolt, I noticed the train was just pulling out of Doncaster station. The train soon gathered speed again and I remember thinking that it would soon be pulling into Halifax, probably in about forty-five minutes or so.

Eventually the train reached Halifax. After getting out I managed to get my kit back on and sling my kit bag across my shoulders. In front of me I faced a flight of stairs that lead me out of the station.

I stepped out of the station and, breathing in a lungful of fresh air, I set off. Walking up Horton Street, I headed for the town centre.

My parents had moved house while I'd been away. My father told me to catch the 24B bus from Market Street. "Get off the bus at Ramsden Street, son, and walk up Ramsden Street. It's the first turning on the left, Rawson Street, number twenty-two, son."

My father's directions were easy for me to follow as I knew where Ramsden Street was.

Finally, I dropped my kit bag outside number twenty-two and knocked on the door. No one answered. I knocked a bit louder, but still no one answered.

Across the street, a neighbour came out. "Won't be back until about 17.30 hrs, son." Looking at my watch, the time was now 16.40. The neighbour called across: "Come in here, lad. I'll make you a cuppa, they won't be long."

"Thank you, that's really nice of you," I called back. "I could just do with a cuppa!"

Mr Parents came back a few minutes before 17.30. I thanked the neighbour again, picked up my kit bag and walked towards number twenty-two. My father came to the door. "By gum lad, didn't expect you until tomorrow! But we're real glad you are here now!"

Mother appeared. She seemed to have a tear in her eye. Probably remembered when Dad arrived home after the war.

Mother whipped me and Dad up some sausages, eggs and chips. I had to admit I was just a bit hungry. It was great sitting with them again.

"What do you think of the army, lad?"

"It's okay, dad, but you will be able to remember the army training from your days; don't reckon it will have changed much. At least now I can drive—we learnt on some three tonners, Bedford K4's."

"I know the ones, Alf, we had those during the war. Fancy still having them now, old crash boxes, eh?"

"Well, they're posting me to Germany after my embarkation leave. Looking forward to that and wondering what it will be like in a working unit, dad."

"You'll be all right lad, you've got the worst over with now."

We talked all evening. "Mind if I have an early night, Mum?

Been travelling since 09.00 hrs this morning."

"Of course, Alf, you go up. Me and dad will clear away."

They let me sleep until 10.00 hrs. First thing I did was to throw on some civvy clothes. Dad had gone to work so I decided to hop into town and have a look around.

Those three weeks just flew by. However, I did see some of my mates, to go for a few drinks, plus I got out on my bike a few times. Visited the Yorkshire Dales a couple of times.

It seemed like no time at all and I was saying goodbye again to my parents. The leave went well and I enjoyed every minute.

Travelling down to London again, I checked through my instructions. Arriving at Kings Cross station I had to get the tube again for Waterloo station. My travel warrant was made out for a place called Borden in Hants.

The train passed through Aldershot. Borden was the next stop. I'd been reunited with some of the lads on that train. The train shuddered to a halt. "All out!" the conductor shouted. We tumbled off the train and looked around. One of the lads shouted: "Well, where the hell are we, is this Borden then?"

The conductor said, "Not quite, lads, it's about three miles up the line, but this is as far as this train goes. Another train will be along in a minute."

It was only a single track and this old train came chugging along. The conductor announced: "Look lads, the Borden Bullet!"

"Why do you think they call it the Borden Bullet, Alf?"

"Don't know, Stan, but I think we are about to find out!"

Once we were seated on the train, the signalman blew his whistle and the train started to pull off. The journey was no more than three miles but it took over half an hour. "We know now, Stan, don't we?" and everyone laughed.

Borden camp in those days was no more than a transit camp—somewhere to hold us until arrangements could be finalised for our embarkation. The camp was a dark, miserable place. The only thing good about it was the NAAF1.

We were only to be there three days and then our journey would begin.

It was 4th June when we moved out. Trucks took us straight into Aldershot where we boarded a train to Waterloo station, London. Then we were transferred to a train bound for Dover. We did, however manage to get some food before the train journey ended.

It was 22.00 hrs and we stood in three ranks on the docks, waiting to embark. It must have taken two hours to get us all on that troop ship. Talk about sardines, in a cabin, fifteen by ten! All twenty-five of us were squeezed in. Hammocks were four berths high with very little room between. None of us slept much that night. The hammocks were swinging to and fro with the movement of the ship. Burt wanted to be sick and a bucket was quickly made available!

In the morning we docked in the Hook of Holland and again it took almost two hours to disembark.

Once we were all off the ship, we were quickly moved onto the train platform. We were impressed—the train looked extremely modern compared to our trains back in England.

A waiter came to each table. "Would you like tea or coffee, boys?" Stan and I ordered tea. The whole journey took eight hours in which time we were served with three excellent meals. "Bloody hell, Alf, talk about first class!" Stan exclaimed with a huge grin on his face. I think most of the lads were pretty excited, chattering and wondering what a working unit consisted of.

As the train was pulling into the station, I noticed the

nameplate on the station—'Herford'. It was when we were helping each other with our packs that we saw them. Stan said, "What the hell is happening?" N.C.O.'s seemed to be popping straight out of the woodwork, all screaming their heads off!

"Right, you lot, grab you kit and get your butts outside! Come on now, move yourselves, come on, move it!"

Chapter Ten

We soon found ourselves clinging on for dear life in the back of those trucks—they were real bone shakers!

Totally confused by now, we were all in a state of shock. Peter Griffiths chimed up: "Is this some kind of bloody joke? Where the hell are they taking us now? Has a war broke out and someone forgot to mention it?" We were all trying to talk over the whirring sound coming from the engines. We were being transported in Austin K5's, and this particular vehicle had this distinctive whirring sound. Someone said that they could be heard coming from three miles off.

After what seemed an age, the trucks pulled up. The N.C.O.'s started up in chorus again, turning the air totally blue once more.

The Corporal shouted: "Get fell in, pick up your dressing, squad, squad, shun, turn right in three's, right turn, quick march, left, right, left, right, swing your bloody arms, if you don't I will snap some of them off and hit you with the soggy ends!" Stan whispered, "Heard that one, Alf," then a voice boomed: "If I catch anyone talking I'll rip his ruddy head off!"

The silly thing was we had only marched a few yards from the trucks and we were halted. We had halted outside two long single story buildings. One of the N.C.O.'s shouted for us to get inside the first building. N.C.O'.s were also inside, directing us to our sleeping quarters. After we had deposited our kit, it was back outside to collect the jolly old bedding again.

Once the bedding exercise was over, we were led into what looked like some kind of lecture room and we were seated. Now a sergeant appeared and introduced himself. "My name is sergeant Hardcastle. You are now all part of the British Troops Column R.A.S.C. You are now in the column training wing. Here you will undergo three weeks continuation training and have a lot to learn about weapons—weapons you will have never seen in basic training and you will be taught everything about them. At the end of this training course you will all have the opportunity to take your number one drill certificate. This weekend we will let you settle in and your training will start on Monday. Just one more thing before we leave you. All webbing equipment will be scrubbed white by Monday morning."

After the sergeant had left we all just looked at one another, dumfounded. Pete said, "Come on, lads, its Friday night now and we've got all weekend. Let's all go up and investigate the NAAFI!"

We all wandered up in two and three's. The NAAFI was pleasant enough and well lit. Stan and I got a drink and a sandwich and found ourselves a seat.

"What do you think, Alf? Bit of a blow, eh?"

"Well Stan, the way I see it, it might be interesting learning about new weapons and, let's face it, the screaming and shouting we're used to. In one ear and out the other, so to speak."

"I suppose you're right Alf, and let's face it, it is only three weeks and we'll definitely be in some working unit. Did you notice the blonde serving, Alf? Not bad, eh? Quite a dish, I'd say, but I'll bet she's some German's lassie."

"Look Stan, I think Bill and Ted are trying to get our attention. Think they want us to make a foursome up at darts?"

"I'm game, Alf—come on."

The evening went down quite well. I think the lads enjoyed themselves. It was taking me a bit of getting used to, all this moving about and different beds, but I slept pretty soundly. I'd gone to sleep thinking of home and determined to get a letter off at the weekend.

Saturday morning I awoke feeling really hungry and couldn't wait to get to the cookhouse. Over breakfast I asked Stan, "What do you fancy doing today?"

"Hadn't given it a lot of thought, Alf."

"Well, some of the lads were thinking about going up into the woods. Well, I suppose it's a forest, really—it goes on for miles."

"Some of the lads were telling Pete last night that there's a place in the woods called Bismarck Tower."

"Now that's a strange place to put a tower, Alf!"

"Yes Stan, but what is even weirder is that apparently

some old gent is there and he sells beer to the lads—Dortmunder Pils. Look, Stan, I don't really feel like a drink in the mornings, so why not let us wander up there after dinner?"

"Okay, Alf, suits me. Why don't we get stuck into scrubbing our webbing white? I'll pop up to the NAAFI and buy a bottle of bleach. That should help remove old Blanco."

The woods were very picturesque, all pine trees, going on for miles. It took us about forty-five minutes to reach Bismarck Tower. Sure enough, the old gent was there. He had crates of beer stacked inside the bottom of the tower. "Eh Stan, we've only got English money!" But surprisingly the old man was only too glad to take English tender. One shilling for a pint of Dortmunder Pils! "That's pretty cheap, Stan!"

Walking back to camp, Stan and I chatted. We had spent a pleasant afternoon and we were both starving, ready for the cookhouse. It was great just being free and having some time to ourselves.

"Tell you what, Stan, how about we have a stroll into Herford in the morning and check it out, like?"

"How far would you say it was, Alf?"

"One of the lads said it was about eight kilometres. A kilometre is five eights of a mile, so by my calculations it works out about five miles."

"Bloody hell, Alf, five miles!"

"It will be a breeze for two old soldiers like us!" Stan laughed and muttered to himself, "A breeze!"

We had a hearty meal in the cookhouse and wandered back to the billet. That evening we just relaxed and listened to Burt's radio.

The following morning after breakfast, we set off. There were four of us—me, Stan, Pete and Bill. We seemed to cover the distance in no time at all.

Herford was a nice sort of place with a splendid park. It was also credited with a YMCA for the British troops, with tearooms and gift shop.

As we were making our way back to camp, Bill shouted: "Eh, have you seen that, lads!" It was only because of Bill's sharp eye; the rest of us would have walked straight past. About a hundred yards to our right we saw it—a military cinema; it was partially screened by those tall pines.

Stan remarked, "Not bad, eh, and it is only about three kilometres from camp. Could stroll down next weekend, Alf."

When we arrived back at the training wing, I suggested to Stan that we check out the notice board. The sergeant pointed out that there would be a training schedule for the next three weeks. According to the schedule, the first two periods were weapons training—the Bren gun (light machine gun) and then drill with the lovable sergeant Hardcastle. The afternoon was a repeat of the mornings training.

"Come on, Stan, grab your eating irons, its chow time!" It was now 12.20 hrs.

Monday morning arrived and once more we were standing outside on parade. We were being inspected by the N.C.O.'s and it was the usual banter: "Soldier, have you shaved this morning? Well may I suggest you bloody well take the paper off the razor blade!"

However, when the N.C.O.'s had had their fun with us, we were split into three groups—two groups of eight and one of nine. "The first group will go with corporal Warboys, the second group with Corporal Rayburn, and finally the last group will be with Corporal Stewart.

"You will remain in your selected groups for the duration of your three weeks training. The N.C.O.'s you have been assigned to will be your weapon training instructors."

We were then taken into the training wing and into separate lecture rooms. As we entered the lecture room there was a Bren gun mounted on a table and three Bren guns spaced out across the lecture room floor. Along one side of the room there were nine chairs. "Now lads, take a seat."

The N.C.O. explained: "The Bren guns have four main parts, the butt groups, and the barrel, tripod and body group. The smallest part on the Bren gun is the barrel locking nut retainer plunger and that tiny part, this bit here," he said, pointing with his finger.

We were then shown how to take the Bren apart and put it back together again. "By the end of this course you will be able to strip the Bren in ten seconds and re-build it in fifteen."

The second period was devoted to learning how to solve breakdowns, like gas stoppages, and get the gun firing again quickly. "You will learn over this course how to solve all the other stoppages than can occur and you will be trained on all these too."

I would not have revealed at this point, to my mates, any of my thoughts, but I found myself intrigued by it all. It was as much of a surprise to me, but I was developing this great interest in weapons and could not wait to discover all the other weapons.

After NAAFI break, sergeant Hardcastle was waiting outside to take us onto the parade ground. Looking back and remembering sergeant Hirst from training, I realised he was a pussycat compared to this Hardcastle fellow! He would march us around that square at a hundred and twenty paces to the minute, plus giving us left and right turns and about turns at the same speed. We all ended up in a right mess! He would pick on some poor soul and send him running around the square with his rifle above his head, then forget about him. I know, because I was one of those poor sods!

After dinner the afternoon was a repeat of the morning. The one thing that was enjoyable was in the lecture room where no shouting took place. I suppose it was a combination of the fresh air and the constant training, but we were starved, always hungry at meal times.

Wednesday was bull night. I supposed it was some kind of tradition in the army. Wednesday evening all the N.C.O.'s would be present to oversee the bullying of the barracks, in preparation of the old man's Thursday morning inspection. In our case it would be for the training wing officer.

Yesterday we had been given more instruction on the Bren gun with further stoppages, and of course, the square bashing on the parade ground.

Today we were introduced to the 3.5 Rocket Launcher. Again, the weapons to me were exciting, but right now it was Bull night.

Thursday's inspection seemed to come and go without a hitch, and now we had got through another gruelling day. We'd been to the cookhouse and had our tea.

With contented stomachs we were relaxing in the billet. I asked Stan, "Fancy going up the NAAFI, maybe get a game of darts or something?"

"Not tonight, Alf. To be honest, I'm a but skint."

"But we will be getting paid tomorrow. Don't bother about that, Stan; come on, tonight I'll stand you a drink."

"You sure, Alf? You know I don't like scrounging."

"Don't be daft, you know that you would do the same for

me, if the shoe was on the other foot! Come on Stan, grab your jacket!"

We headed straight to the NAAFI. When we entered the music was blasting away from the jukebox. Burt and Pete were seated over the other side.

"Come on Stan, we'll see if they want to make up a foursome."

The following morning we were on pay parade, with no idea how we were going to be paid. It came as a surprise when we were handed this paper money. It was just like monopoly money. "They called this money, Stan" We had three-penny notes, six penny, a shilling and so on up to a pound. The only coinage was a half penny and a penny. This money could only be spent in the NAAFI, YMCA's and the cinema. If we wished to have German money, we could, but it would have to be requested in advance.

Both Stan and I walked off the pay parade with a wad of notes. We thought we were rich!

In the week that followed, we just about covered the rest of the weapons. These included the Bren gun, Sten gun, the Lea-Enfield rifle, grenades and the 3.5 Rocket launcher, an anti-tank weapon. My mind was full of it. I really enjoyed the weapon side of the training.

But now we were in our final week. Again we were being brushed up for the inevitable forthcoming passing out parade.

To qualify for our number one drill certificate, each one of us had to drill the squad for about ten minutes, give them turnings on the march and making sure the order to turn was given on the correct foot.

In the lecture room, again, we had to instruct the squad in a weapon of the instructor's choice. I think everyone passed the tasks they had set for us. The quality of instruction was not as good as the N.C.O.'s but we were graded on standard.

Then it came to the final passing out parade. By this time, we had gained our confidence, but I do think that most of the lads had remembered the words of sergeant Hirst: "Bags of swank, lads!" Those few whispered words had stuck with us.

On the Saturday morning on parade, sergeant Hardcastle informed us which company we were being allocated to.

Stan and I were being split up. He was being sent to a place called Bielefeld, to 118 Company, and I was staying in Herford. I was going to 138 Company, field ambulance. We were both a bit upset. We had been through everything from day one. However, I think we were half expecting it.

We were both being sent to the relevant company after dinner. Four other lads where going with Stan and transport was being laid on for them at 14.00 hrs.

Chapter Eleven

138 Company field ambulances. The company consisted of six platoons. Each one was broken down into seven sections. Our company commander's name was a Major Briggs. Each platoon had an officer—ours was a lieutenant Drake. Then we had two lovable sergeants, a sergeant Williams and a sergeant Wiles. One was our MT sergeant and the other one was our Admin sergeant.

Each section had a section commander, a full corporal and a lance corporal was his second in command.

I'd tagged on with a lad called Jim Longstaff. We hit if off straight away. He was a National Serviceman and married but we soon bonded as great friends.

What I liked about being in a working unit was that we were always on exercises. Sometimes these manoeuvres would last for weeks.

They began to take us all over Germany, Minden, Osnabruck, Munster and further south to Dusseldorf and Monchengladbach. The list was endless. Germany I found was quite beautiful.

A typical exercise involved the whole company driving to a map reference. We would usually be in a wood were we would scrim up and then dig defensive slit trenches.

From this base each section would be dispersed to separate map references and make camp. The corporal would then send each one of us back to headquarters with slips of paper. The papers would relate how many wounded—imaginary bodies of supposedly wounded men. We were supposed to be ferrying wounded men from the front lines.

It was after one of these exercises and we were returning to camp. As I drove through the camp gates a military policeman was stopping each vehicle. When it got to me—"Your name driver Cartwright?"

"Yes corporal."

"Then park up and get over to the sergeant major's office. The old man wants to see you the moment you have returned!"

As I parked up, Jim was just climbing out of his ambulance. "What's up Alf?"

"Don't know Jim, but the old man wants to see me straight away."

The sergeant major marched me into the major's office.

"Sit down lad!"

"I'd rather not, sir, I'm a bit dirty, just come back from exercise."

"Sit down, son," he insisted. "I've got some bad news for

you, son. There's no easy way for me to tell you, but I'll come right to the point. Your father was killed this morning. I don't have any details right now but travel warrants have been made out for you. You are going home tomorrow. You will be given seven days compassionate leave. Now go off lad and pack whatever you think you will need."

I wandered back to the billet in a kind of daze.

Once back in the billet, Jim came over. "What's the matter Alf?"

"My father was killed this morning, Jim. I'm off tomorrow—compassionate leave."

"I'm so sorry, Alf. Look, let me take you for a drink tonight. I know you probably wont feel like it but I think you need it."

"I can't believe all this, Jim, can't believe it has happened. Only came home from the war ten years ago… I *will* have that drink tonight."

In the NAAFI that night, a chap came over to us. "Alf, I'm taking you to the station in the morning. We're going in the old man's Land Rover. Your train departs at 09.15 hrs. Glad I caught you, Alf, you will need to go to breakfast early. Can you wait outside the guardroom at 08.30 hrs? See you in the morning then."

Jim and I looked at each other. "Looks like you will be off early then. Hope you find your family bearing up. I'll be thinking of you and I'm sure most of the lads will be."

The train journey was like before. Three square meals. The train pulled into the Hook of Holland at exactly 15.00 hrs to connect with the afternoon ferry. It was a bit different to the troopship we had previously arrived in. Most of the journey I spent on deck just looking over the side.

When we were about five miles offshore, you could just

make out the white cliffs of Dover. I remember thinking, Did my father have this same view when he was coming home? I would have given anything to have had him standing next to me right then, just to talk to him.

We were soon disembarking at Dover. The sun was still shining from a clear blue sky. To all outside appearances it was a wonderful day.

The train to take me to London was standing on platform three. This would take me to Waterloo station and I would have to take the tube to Kings Cross. The final part of my journey would take me to Halifax. The flying Scotsman pulled in on platform twelve and I got on board.

Looking at my watch, it was 19.45 hrs. The journey should take about four hours. That would get me into Halifax before 24.00 hrs.

It would make it a long walk home from town but I couldn't see mother going to bed early that night.

Walking home that night I will always remember. My thoughts were for my parents. I wondered how my mother was coping. It must have knocked her sideways when the news was first broken to her. I wished I could have been there for her. Now I was picturing my father and how we had talked on that last morning before I left. The last words my father spoke to me were: "Son, be a good soldier." Well, I dammed well was going to be. I'd get some of those stripes on my arm, if only for my father's memory.

When I approached the street, it was quiet and dark. I walked silently up the street and gently knocked on the door, so as not to disturb the neighbours. My sister opened the door. "Come in, Alf, I've sent mother to bed—she was exhausted. Let's both go to bed now." I agreed

In the morning my sister was cooking breakfast.

"Have the arrangements been made, Elsie?" I asked.

"Yes, the funeral will take place on Friday. Dad's being cremated."

"I don't like that. Dad should have a decent burial."

"It was the funeral director's suggestion. Mother was in a state."

"Well, what's done is done I suppose, but if I had been here, it would have been different."

The funeral took place at the funeral home, on Clare Road. Most of my parents' family came from Bradford and Leeds and because of this a sit-down meal had been arranged with the Co-op.

My uncle Alf attended the funeral. He was some sort of hero, in the last war. He had joined the Green Howards at sixteen, giving a false age. He went on and worked his way through the ranks and finally took a commission, coming out after twelve years as a Captain, plus a military medal for bravery.

We did manage to snatch a few words together before he left. He asked me how I was finding army life. I told him: "Fine, Uncle, it's getting better now with the basic training behind me."

"Well, son, if you are like me you will love it, but I don't think I would like being an officer in peace time. There's too much paperwork. Sergeant—that's the rank, Alf. I loved being a sergeant before my commission. Above that and it means a lot of paperwork."

Soon the family had all left, and mother and I were left alone. "Don't start worrying yourself over me, son, I'm made of pretty strong stuff. The hardest bit for me was getting the funeral over. I'll be all right now."

That week soon seemed to pass and I found myself travelling back again to Germany. When I arrived back at camp, Jim was seated on his bed bulling his boots. "Eh, Jim, missed me?"

"Not half! Sergeant Williams has been up to his old tricks again—well, he's got two of us to pick on now!"

As the story went, Sergeant Williams had married a lass and she had run off with some Geordie fellow and this Williams had taken an instant dislike to Jim because he was from Newcastle. That was the crux of the matter and me being his friend meant that I would get it in the neck too.

Jim said, "One day Alf, that Williams will get his comeuppance and wouldn't I just love to be there!"

"Come on Jim, put those boots down—let's go down to the NAAFI, the drinks are on me."

Jim was always skint but sometimes he was sent money from home, and then he would treat me. Being a National Serviceman, his family were aware that he would be struggling to manage on ten bob a week. Every now and then they would send him something.

Jim seemed genuinely pleased that I was back. On Sunday we decided to take a walk into Badsazuflen, a small town in the opposite direction to Herford. It was a pleasant walk, about three miles; when I look back now, it was a beautiful town. The sun was shining. One thing about Germany—the weather seemed guaranteed in the summer, with endless sunshine.

I'd been back in the camp about five weeks when the news came.

Chapter Twelve

The Major had gathered everyone into the cookhouse.

"Wonder what this is all about, Alf?"

"I've a bit of an idea, Jim," I said. "I've been keeping an eye on the newspapers."

The Major spoke for the first time: "All the training you men have undergone is going to be put into practice. Some man calling himself Nassa has decided to seize the Suez Canal! A treaty was drawn up after the war regarding the Suez Canal that it would always be kept open for world shipping. Now this Nassa has taken it on himself to put up a blockade there. Obviously, he thinks that he can tell all of us what to do, but our Prime Minister, Sir Anthony Eden, says differently. He is immobilising the British Army and sending us all out there. Now, boys, time is crucial for us! We are expecting orders any day now which will put us on twenty-four hours standby. I know that I can count on every single one of you men. All the vehicles will have to be thoroughly cleaned in preparation for painting. Yes, each vehicle will have to be painted yellow to blend in with the sand – you can all imagine the scale of the work involved here. You will all be working round the clock on sixteen-hour shifts. Plus, all the vehicles will have to be fully serviced to get them in tip-top condition. Remember, boys, when you do get out there, the Arabs can steal the shirt off your backs: they are bigger thieves than 'C' platoon!" That brought a laugh. "This is what most of you boys joined up for—to see some action! So let's get our sleeves rolled up and get stuck in!"

While the old man was talking, my mind flashed back to when I was standing in the recruitment office on the 8th February. When the recruitment sergeant pressed a shilling into my hand and said, "That's the Queen's shilling, lad," I suppose that is what it was—for Queen and Country, like.

Over the next few days, a large number of reservists had been called up. This was to build up the strength of each company. Despatch riders had been coming in and out of the guardroom day and night. This was continuous.

Six days had passed since the old man had addressed us all. Now orders had come through for the advance party to move out. 118 company and column HQ were the advance party.

They started moving out of camp at 09.00 hrs on the 21st September 1956 bound for Amsterdam. This was their stopover point, while they waited for ships to take them to the Middle East.

The camp seemed deserted, just our Company and a detachment of R.E. being left. The queues in the NAAFI and the cookhouse were not quite as long. However, we were busy. We had continuous exercises; these were carried out over a five-mile radius in and around the surrounding woods. It was on one of those exercises that things got a little out of hand.

We were supposed to run a convoy of ambulances through the woods. The officer in charge told us it was vital that the convoy got through. We had to treat the exercise like active service. This proved to be our downfall. The reservists were the enemy and they had to stop the convoy at all costs. Playing their part, they became a little over enthusiastic.

Jim and I were driving through the woods when we saw a soldier standing on the side of the track. "Pull over Jim, he's one of ours." It was Bill. "What happened, Bill?"

"They are bloody crazy, Alf! They just dragged us out of the ambulances and set about us with great lumps of wood! Pete's lying over there in the edge where they left him. I think he's unconscious."

"Bloody hell, there's no need for that! Come on, let's get him into the ambulance. You get him with Bill. This is one ambulance that's going to get through!"

Eventually we cleared the woods and headed straight for the military hospital, bypassing the camp. We wanted to have Pete checked out. He was just coming round and his neck was killing him, just as we reached the gates of the hospital. He was badly bruised and shaken but no bones broken.

We arrived back at camp and reported in. The officer demanded to know just where we'd been. We told him the whole story without leaving anything out. "But we did get through, Sir."

"Yes, you did the right thing, men, but you lads were not the only casualties this afternoon. The first aid room has been busy patching your mates up."

We'd all been moved about a bit in the barracks. Burt and I ended up sharing a room with two of the reservists. One of them was a gypsy; everyone took him to be a bit crazy. None of the N.C.O.'s could do anything with him—he would just lie on his bed all day long. He had come in to fight, not to clean brasses or polish boots.

It was on a Sunday morning when Burt spoke to me. "Alf, can I confide in you?"

"Sure Burt, what is it?"

"Alf, I'm really terrified. It's the gypsy. He comes to me during the night and puts a knife to my throat and talks real close to me. I can smell his breath and it stinks. He tells me that he would like to stick the knife in me, to see what happens!"

"Eeh, come on Burt, we must tell someone now!"

It must have been sheer coincidence when the knock came at the door. "I'll answer that, Burt."

Two guys where standing there looking for the gypsy. "How are you boys getting on with our gypsy friend?"

Burt just let it all spill out. The two men were reservists from the signal barracks across the road. They both looked at poor Burt.

"My name is Neil," one of them introduced himself. "Look, lads, when the gypsy comes back, tell him Neil has been to see him and that if he gives you any trouble, he will be back and will sort him and his sidekick out. I don't go along with bullying, not me."

The gypsy and his friend got back to the billet around 17.00 hrs just before teatime. We were just about to leave for the cookhouse. Burt blurted it all out and said, "He said that he would sort you both out if there was any more trouble." The gypsy turned on his heel, not saying a word and lay down on his bed.

Burt never had any more trouble.

Six weeks had passed by since the advance party had left. Now they were coming back. Nassa had backed down and the Suez Canal was open again for world shipping. The reservists were being sent back home.

Things were now getting back to normal. However, we were faced with the task of repainting all the vehicles to their original colours. The Suez crisis was history.

Jim and I were now thinking of leave. We were allowed six weeks leave a year to the UK. The two of us decided to split the six weeks into two three-week periods and put in for February. It would then be twelve months since we both joined the army. "Just imagine, Jim, three long weeks with your wife!"

"Yes," he agreed, "it's something to look forward to."

Jim had moved back into our billet with the reservists gone.

"Fancy going up to the NAAFI, Alf, for a few drinks and maybe a game of darts?" he suggested. "Bill, Pete, fancy coming with us?"

They both retorted in unison: "Why not!" We all left the billet together.

Yes, things were getting back to normal. The exercises we'd come to enjoy were back. Those next few months began to fly and it was February. We were both excited about our leave now. We both felt we had been away for years. So much had happened this last twelve months.

Jim's leave was on the same date as mine, which meant we could travel together as far as London. It couldn't have worked out better. "Suppose you've told the little lady, Jim, or is it to be a surprise?"

"Sure, she would never forgive me if I hadn't."

"Just think, Jim, instead of going home on leave we were nearly on troopships to the Middle East. That was a bit of luck!"

"Yes, Alf, I just want to do my National Service without hiccups and go home for good."

When I finally reached home, mother seemed to be more like her old self—cheerful like. It was good to be home for three weeks. One thing I'd missed was mother's Yorkshire puddings. I hadn't had one in twelve months. They were something kind of special on a Sunday.

It was Saturday now and I'd managed to contact some of my mates. We'd planned to meet at the Victoria Hall. It was great to see my old friends again.

Now, walking home that night, I had decided to call at the fish shop. It was about halfway home and I would enjoy them all the more, eating them out of the paper. Entering the fish shop, I saw her—she was absolutely beautiful! Small, about five feet tall, slim, and her hair was long, dark and shiny. She was standing with a girl I immediately recognised. She used to live next door to me, Barbara Anderson. They were obviously together.

"Hello, Barbara, going to introduce me to your friend?"

"This is Maureen, Alf."

"Pleased to meet you, Maureen!"

That week I checked on Barbara's parents just to say hello, like. Well, that was my excuse! On the following Friday, my luck was in. Maureen was at Mrs Anderson's.

By the end of the evening, I'd plucked up enough courage to ask Maureen: "Tell you what, Maureen, how about if I walk you home?"

"Sure Alf, that's nice of you." During the walk, we made arrangements to go to the cinema together.

The last two weeks of my leave we spent quite a lot of time together. I did find out in the short time, that Maureen was on the rebound. She'd just broken up with her last boyfriend, so I wasn't going to count chickens yet. However, it would be nice to have someone to write to and just to see what develops.

When I finally left home I remember boarding the train at Halifax and feeling elated. I'd met a wonderful girl on my leave.

I finally arrived at Dover, waiting for the Ferry. As luck would have it, I bumped into Jim. "It couldn't have worked out better, Jim! At least we can travel back to Germany together."

When we reached camp, we settled down in the billet. Pete came over to us. "Look, lads, Burt has had some rotten news."

"What's the matter, Pete?"

"Burt's had a Dear John."

"That's bloody awful, Pete." We knew what a 'Dear John' was—we'd seen it many times before. Some poor guy's girlfriend had met someone else. "He must be feeling pretty bad."

"Yes, he's taking it hard. What I want to ask you lads is, how about all of us taking Burt into Herford tonight and getting him drunk? It will take him out of himself and show him he's got real friends."

We did take Burt out that night and, yes, we did get him drunk! The three of us managed to get him back to camp and got him tucked up in bed.

Jim and I had been back about three weeks. We'd been

looking on 'part one' orders. In the army, we had learnt that you had to keep a check on part one orders. My name was up there—I was on company orders to report to the major on Monday morning.

"What's that all about, Jim?" I said, bemused. "I don't think I've done anything wrong!"

Chapter Thirteen

The following morning I was excused working parade. I was allowed time off to get myself ready for O.C.'s orders. Having checked my dress, brasses and boots, I set off for the Company HQ, reporting to the sergeant major's office. He inspected me before marching me into the old man's office. "Left right, left right, right wheel, mark time, halt, left turn!"

The commanding officer said, "Stand at ease, driver!" After a moment, he continued: "Someone in the column training wing seems to think very highly of you, son. You have been selected for a N.C.O.'s course. You will report to the column training wing at 08.00 hrs on Monday morning with full kit. What do you thinks of that, driver Cartwright?"

"I am very pleased, Sir."

"Well, somehow I think you will do very well on this

course. Dismiss!"

"Left turn, left right, left right, right wheel, halt, dismiss, driver—now report to your platoon."

When I got outside I said to myself, "Well, blow me, this is a turn up for the books and no mistake!"

Walking onto the vehicle park I spotted Jim. I told him what the old man had said.

"N.C.O.'s course, eh, Alf!" Jim smiled. "Well, you deserve it. It's about time something good happened to one of us."

"Yes, but it will mean going through it all again in the training wing. No doubt the nice sergeant Hardcastle will be there to give me a hug!"

"Alf, it's nothing to worry about, you can do the drill standing on your head! As for the weapons, well, I know how much you love handling the weapons."

"What makes you say that, Jim?"

"Alf, when we were in the training wing the first time, I saw your face light up every time it was weapon training!"

"Guess I didn't fool you, did I, Jim!"

"You seem to have a flair for weapons, Alf. Anyone can see that. Give it your best shot, Alf!"

"Eh, come on Jim, it's time for NAAFI break time!"

Jim and I had our usual four sausage rolls and a pot of tea. The jukebox was blaring out a song called 'Happy Days are Here Again!' It seemed a popular song at that time and the lads seemed to be giving it some stick. Someone seemed to be playing it every time we stepped into the NAAFI!

We were soon back on the vehicle park, working on Jim's ambulance. Jim had a service coming up. Whenever one of the lads had a service coming up, the rest of the lads would all work on that particular ambulance. We used to get a can with petrol and oil in it and wash all the underside of the ambulance until it gleamed.

That was the routine between exercises, so that all the vehicles were kept in tiptop condition—especially since we never really knew when the next exercise would be.

Back in the billet that evening Jim said, "Come on, Alf, I'll give you a hand with bulling your kit up over the weekend. You know what it will be like in the training wing—bull, bull and more bull! It will give you a flying start for Monday, like."

"You're a good mate, Jim!"

"You'd do the same for me, Alf, if the boot was on the other foot."

About 21.00 hrs I said, "Come on, Jim, let's go up to the NAAFI. I'll buy you a pint—you deserve it!"

The following morning was Saturday. We decided to take a stroll up to the Bismarck Tower in the woods. On the walk back, we decided to rest on a nice grassy slope. The sun was beating down. The birds were singing. It was so peaceful out there, far from the bustle of the camp. It always gave me a roaring appetite for when we got back to camp.

But for the time Jim and I lay there taking in the sun, and my thoughts strayed to Monday and the beginning of the N.C.O. training course. I was quite excited.

I was the only one selected from my company for the course. The rest of the lads had been selected from other companies scattered around Germany.

It was about 10.00 hrs on that Monday morning before all the students had arrived. There were twenty-four of us altogether. I, with seven others, had been assigned to Corporal Rayburn for weapons training. Apparently it had been said that

Corporal Rayburn was the finest instructor in the training wing, so I had been fortunate. Of course, the loveable sergeant Hardcastle would be taking us on the square for drill. From the outset I decided to do my utmost to do well on this course. I was after that promotion and this was my opportunity.

About halfway through the course I had a word with Corporal Rayburn. "Excuse me, Corporal Rayburn, what chances are there of me borrowing some of the weapons' manuals, to study, like, in the evenings?"

"Nobody has ever asked to borrow manuals—it must be a first! Come on, I'll lend you my personal set, but look after them now. It's refreshing to see someone so keen!"

I remember back then, one of the lads had a single record player; it reminded me of Burt's radio in training, but this time it was worse—we only had one record, 'Rock Around the Clock' by Bill Hayley, and this was played continuously!

However, there were times when we would escape to the NAAFI in the evenings. It gave me the opportunity to see Jim and to keep him up to date on how things were going.

Inspections were on a daily basis. I remember one of these inspections in particular. Sergeant Hardcastle had come strolling down the billets room waving his pay stick. He suddenly stopped by my bed. He placed his pay stick inside one of my boots and lifted it up from the bed. Before I'd realised what was happening, my boot was flying through the air. I cringed every time it contacted with something. What was going through my mind in that instant was all the polish would be cracking! Months of bull ruined in a few seconds! I would have to start all over again from scratch. The only word Hardcastle uttered when the boot was flying through the air was 'SHIT!'

Two days before the end of the course our practical exams

were taken on the parade ground and in the lecture room. Then it was ultimately completed with the passing out parade on the Saturday morning.

No one was given the course results. We all had to wait until we arrived back at our respective companies.

That following Monday morning I was standing outside the old man's office waiting for the company sergeant major to march me in. Moments later I was standing in front of the old man.

As he looked up at me, he was grinning from ear to ear. "Jolly good show, jolly good show, driver! You are a credit to your Company. You have come top on the N.C.O.'s course—number one, son, number one! The R.S.M., the adjutant and the training wing officer, they have all recommended immediate promotion to Lance Corporal. Myself, well, I am delighted—well done! Now go and get that stripe on your arm, you are improperly dressed! Dismiss!"

The Company sergeant major then marched me out. "Just one moment, Corporal." It seemed strange being addressed as corporal for the first time.

The sergeant major took me into his office. "Now then, son, now you have got your first stripe, you do nothing and when you get your second, you do even less. From now on son, you delegate!"

I don't think, for one moment, that the company sergeant had meant that literally, that I would have the authority to delegate. It was good to have the course behind me now. It was good to be back with the lads.

Standing out on parade, the following morning felt different, especially when the M.T. sergeant called me out. "Corporal Cartwright, you will be with number three section." This did me fine. It meant that Jim and I would still be in the same section. Sergeant Williams wasn't too happy—he still kept having digs at Jim, but now he would have to be more careful.

I was determined that this stripe would not make a lot of difference to my friendship with Jim or, in fact, with any of my friends. I would still get under the vehicles and get my sleeves rolled up. In fact, one of the other N.C.O.s commented on this one day:

"Alf, did I see you under a truck this morning?"

"Yes George, you did."

"But you don't really have to now."

"I know, George, but the lads respect me all the more for it. They would do anything for me and I find that they work that little bit harder when the see an N.C.O. getting his hands dirty. You should give it a try, George; maybe they won't skive off quite as much!"

"Well, you might have a point, Alf. I'm always looking for one of them."

The months that followed went smoothly. Once you allowed yourself to settle, army life wasn't too bad. However, it was easy for me to talk—I was a regular and with the pay increase and promotion, my pay got me over £4. Some of the National Service lads were still struggling on ten shillings.

Behind each of their locker was a calendar and each day would be ticked off. All they ever talked about was their next leave and when the final day would come. No, if a man didn't like the army life, it could be sheer hell, believe me!

Tonight was Friday. "Fancy a bit of supper up the NAAFI, Jim?"

"Chance would be a fine thing, Alf. I'm skint as usual!"

"Don't be like that, Jim! The supper is on me."

Jim lost the argument and we went to the NAAFI. When we entered, the jukebox was blasting out another popular tune. It went something like this: 'Run to the station, jump on the train, march at the double down lover's lane, then in the glen'—and so on. Quite lively, it was. Blondie was serving behind the counter that evening. "Eh, Blondie, two sausage and chips for Jim and I!"

"Nothing else, lads?"

"Aye, that's all, Blondie."

"You want an egg then?"

"No, just sausage and chips."

Blondie started to go red in the face. One of the other lads that had been standing in the queue jumped in. "She thinks you are pulling her leg. 'Aye' sounds like 'Eye', which in German means egg!"

We all looked at each other and burst out laughing. Even Blondie saw the funny side.

One of the lads started on the piano in the corner. We all started singing some of the old tunes from the last war. It turned out to be a real cracking night.

Yes, time had been passing quickly. Jim and I would soon be setting off on leave again shortly. Jim's leave was to start on the first week in June. This was 1957. My leave wasn't until the third week, the 22nd to be exact. This time we weren't able to travel together.

"You can't win them all, Jim!"

"No, but we can bloody well try!"

Maureen hadn't been a right good letter writer but she did seem pleased that I was coming home. The weather was great, too—one of those long hot summers I mentioned earlier, which seemed to be the norm in Germany.

That leave Maureen and I got engaged. It was on June 28th. I'd bought the ring form Ballentines Jewellers in the town. It had three stones. I remember that morning, clearly. Maureen was going to work and I'd set off with her. We were both standing in this bus shelter. "Maureen, what do you think of this then?"—and I showed her the ring.

"It's lovely, Alf!"

"Well, put it on then, see if it fits, like!"

The ring fitted Maureen's finger perfectly. "Well, that's it, lass, we are now officially engaged!" I managed to put my arms around her and gently kissed her on the lips, before the bus came.

The leave seemed to pass quickly, it always did. But I wasn't bothered—I'd had a smashing, meaningful leave. I was happy with the world.

I arrived back at camp on the 13th June. I remember just walking through the camp gates when someone shouted my name. Looking up I saw George. He was one of the N.C.O.'s in my platoon. "Come on up to the NAAFI, Alf—have I got some news for you! I'd been told to look out for you arriving back. Something really important has come up. First, let's get a beer in our hands!"

Once we had settled, George began to talk. "When we leave here, I've to help you get all your kit from 'C' block. We're both moving into the training wing tonight and the adjutant wants to see you in the morning."

Chapter Fourteen

"George, what's all this about, moving into the training wing tonight?"

"It's straight up, Alf, and the adjutant wants to see you first thing in the morning."

"Come on, George, what's the big secret?"

"Look, Alf, I'm not supposed to say anything, was told to keep stum, but I will tell you anyway, its no big deal. On Saturday morning you and me are heading back to Blighty. We're going to a place called Hythe; it's on the south coast. Apparently, there is a place there called 'The School of Infantry'. We will undergo an eight weeks' course in weapons; at the end of the course we will be qualified instructors and I believe you will be promoted to full corporal for the course."

"Wow, that's a real turn up, but why us?"

"They told me I had been chosen because I had come

number one on a drill course. I'm guessing that you must have done something similar."

"Yes, I did come top of the course I attended a few months ago. Well, that question has been answered. Look, George, I'm going to have another pint—same for you?"

"Why not, Alf!"

"You do know what tonight is, don't you, George? It's Thursday—bull night—and sergeant Williams will be overseeing the bulling."

"It's okay, Alf, he can't stop us—the orders are straight from the adjutant."

When we entered 'C' block, sure enough sergeant Williams was screaming down the corridor: "You two grab a bumper and start polishing the floor!"

"Sorry sergeant, but me and George here are moving out—we're moving into the training wing tonight."

"Rubbish! Grab that ruddy bumper!"

"Look, Sergeant Williams, it's the adjutant's orders. If you would like to take it up with him in the morning, okay?"

Williams was standing there seething and going redder and redder in the face, but he knew he would have to let us move out.

The following morning I was marched before the adjutant. The adjutant more or less told me what George had said the previous evening. The adjutant seemed quite pleased when he was telling me to put another stripe up. "If you successfully pass this course, Corporal Cartwright, you will keep this second stripe and you will be paid all the relevant back pay. This weekend, Corporal Rayburn and Corporal Warboys will be going over all the weapons with you both. Monday morning you will be setting off for England. Your train leaves Herford station at 09.00 hrs. It will be necessary for you both to take full kit on this course. Dismiss!"

Saturday morning George and I managed to get to the cookhouse early, about 07.00 hrs. We were both a bit excited. Later we helped one another put our packs on.

"Seems daft, George, having to take this lot!"

"Yes, we'll probably not need most of it."

Transport had been arranged for us, to take us to the station in Herford. We had been told to be outside the guardroom by 8.15 hrs. The Austin K5 pulled up exactly on time. "Come on George, let's get on board!" The moment the K5 pulled off George and I had to cling onto something for dear life! It was impossible to sit down with all our kit on.

I don't know why, but all German railway stations seemed to smell of cigars. The Germans did seem to prefer to smoke cigars. George and I thought it was more likely because they couldn't make decent cigarettes in Germany. From our experience, all the Germans we had met, seemed keen to buy our cigarettes, English ones, that is.

George and I had a pleasant journey on the train and ferry. Everything seemed to go without a hitch. That is, until we reached Dover.

George said, "Come on, Alf, if we're lucky through the customs, we'll be able to get the connecting train for London. If we miss it, it will mean a three-hour wait until the next."

As we both approached the customs, George went in front of me. "Have you anything to declare?" George replied with a curt "No". His kit bag was quickly marked with chalk and George passed through the barrier. Now it was my turn.

"Have you anything to declare, son?"

"No Sir."

"Could you please unpack your kit bag then?"

"Rather not sir, it took me over an hour to pack it this morning. Tight as a drum, it is. Feel free to unpack it, sir, but you will have to re-pack it again."

With that the customs officer ignored my kit bag and proceeded to search my webbing. "Can't understand you lads coming into the country and having nothing to declare."

"Like I said, sir, not going on leave, going on a course so there's a difference." After a while the officer gave up. Marking my kit bag he said, "On you way, Corporal."

I had missed that connecting train to London. I thought George would be well on his way by now. It meant I would now be arriving in Hythe three hours after George. What the heck, I thought, what's a few hours to me? I decided to look around and see if there was somewhere I could get a hot cup of tea and a sandwich. I had now two and a half hours to kill.

Arriving at Waterloo station, it was just a matter of changing platforms. Soon I was climbing on board the train that would take me to Hythe.

It was quite a pleasant journey. I was enjoying the scenery looking out of the window. It was beautiful. It reminded me of the Dales—the only difference was it was quite flat. The journey from London to Hythe only took about an hour and half.

Once I arrived at the station in Hythe, I thought it would be best to ask someone local. There was an elderly gentleman walking just in front of me as we came out of the station.

"Excuse me, sir," I said, "I wondered if you could possibly give me some directions. I'm looking for a place called School of Infantry."

"With all that kit on, son, you would be better off catching the bus! Come on, I happen to be catching the same bus, number 47."

While we were waiting for the bus we got talking. "So you want to become a weapon training instructor?" the old gent said. "I've lived here for most of my life, son, and the place you are going to has been turning out instructors since before the war. They've been turning out the finest instructors in the world and that's a fact. You will be all right there. This is your stop coming up—come on, I'll take your kit bag."

As I stepped off the bus, the old gent passed me down the kit bag and wished me all the best on my course.

Looking around, I couldn't miss the camp entrance on the opposite side of the road. Above the entrance were the words 'The School of Infantry' in large letters. The first thing was to report to the guardroom. In the guardroom was a strapping six-foot sergeant nearly as broad as he was tall. However, he was a big cheerful guy.

"Come on, son, I'll point you in the right direction," he said.

The camp wasn't large but very compact. The billets seemed to be all down the right-hand side. Set back on the left I could pick out the NAAFI and the cookhouse. The sergeant pointed out Hut 27 on the right.

"That's where you will be billeted, son, for the whole of the course."

Thanking the sergeant, I headed for Hut 27. The first face I clapped eyes on was George.

He was stretched out on his bed. When he saw me he just grinned. "What kept you Alf? I thought you was behind me at customs! I got on the train and waited for you. When you didn't turn up I guessed that some customs guy had decided to stop and search you. Well, you're here now—come on, just throw your kit on the bed and let's go up to the NAAFI. I'll bet you are as dry as a board!"

Once we were settled in the NAAFI with a steaming hot mug of coffee, George spoke first. "Haven't been able to check out the cookhouse yet, but I believe tea will be about the usual time, 17.00 hrs. We can check out Hythe if you like. We've still got a couple of hours before teatime. Really, the time is our own till Monday morning."

We both lit a cigarette and enjoyed our coffee. "Wonder what this course will be like, George? At least there will be no square bashing and bulling our kit will be kept to a minimum. Their main objective will be to make instructors out of us. I'm looking forward to this particular course. I've been fascinated with weapons since training. Can't believe my luck getting on a course like this. They say it's a good course to have behind you."

"I feel just the same about weapons as you, Alf. Come on, let's see what Hythe has to offer. We'll see where the hub of the town is."

There was a large café-come-restaurant. Some of the lads from the camp seemed to have found it already. Apparently, there was a small dance hall, a cinema and one or two quiet little pubs. The only thing I wasn't keen on was the beaches— all shingle, no soft sand like Blackpool that I was used to. I thought I'd take Maureen to Blackpool on my next leave. For me, I like a beach where I can stretch out on, something I can't do on shingle.

We spent about an hour in Hythe. It was only a small seaside town. Before long it was time to make our way back to Camp and see what the cookhouse was like.

Chapter Fifteen

The following morning after breakfast, we were told to stand fast in the cookhouse. The commanding officer was going to give us a talk. The cookhouse seemed to be the appropriate place as we were all together, so to speak.

"Men, welcome to the School of Infantry. We hope you enjoy your stay. When you finally do leave here in eight weeks, you will have the pleasure of knowing that you are Hythe trained. Be proud, men, because this is the finest training camp in the world. You have all been specially chosen from your selected regiments to attend this course. So with lots of hard work you will all do well and attain high grades here at Hythe."

The major then turned and walked off. The instructors now took over and we were divided into groups of twelve and designated our instructor for the entire course.

George and I soon began to realise this was a senior N.C.O.'s course. Out of the 120 that had attended this course, at least 100 of them were sergeants, most of which were near sergeants. You could see that most of them had just been promoted to attend this course and hadn't had time to whiten their stripes.

"Bloody hellfire, Alf, I think that me and you have joined the wrong lot! Just think, if we had joined the goddamn infantry we too would have been attending this course with three stripes on our arms. Just shows how tight our lot are."

"Never mind, George, maybe our turn will come later."

George and I found the course really interesting, especially when they introduced a new weapon to us. It was the sub-machine carbine. It hadn't been released fully into the army as yet. It was to replace the old Sten gun, a weapon designed for close quarter combat.

Over the weeks that were to follow, we did have the opportunity to fire all the weapons we were being instructed on. One Wednesday morning we were taken onto the ranges to fire the Bren gun. I am certain that this morning's exercise was designed to test our stamina and our endurance. They started us off at 600 yards from the targets, and were told to fire off ten live rounds at the targets. At this point, the targets were about the size of a shilling; then we were run flat out down to the 500 yards point.

Again, we had to repeat by firing another ten rounds off at the target. At least the target did seem to be getting bigger, but that bleeding Bren gun which weighed twenty eight pounds, seemed to be getting heavier for every one hundred yards we ran with it. We didn't get any breather; soon as we had fired off the ten rounds, we were up and running again.

By the time we had reached the 200 yards point, the Bren gun seemed to weigh a ton. As regards hitting the target, I don't think we could have hit a barn door. Our breathing was ragged and the breathing control exercises we had been taught were completely out of the window.

The rocket launcher fired an HE-AT rocket. The HE-AT was an abbreviation for high explosive anti-tank rocket. This rocket, when fired, could be seen travelling through its flight. Its speed was only 280ft per second. The remarkable thing about this weapon was that the moment the rocket was fired from the launcher; pressure began to build up inside the rocket. On impact, the pressure would be so intense, it could burn a hole through armoured steel, a hole no larger than the size of an old penny.

It was actually the tank's own explosive which would be ignited by the rocket, then *boom*, the tank would be disabled. Consequently all the enemy crew would perish.

One of the worst scenarios out of all the weapons was the 36 Mills grenade. I actually felt sorry for the bomb disposal officer. He would have to go out and disarm the grenades which hadn't exploded. George said on that particular morning: "That officer, Alf, has got some guts, real guts. I could not do his job for all the tea in China."

That evening while we were in the cookhouse having our tea, George said, "One of the lads is looking for someone to go out on a double date."

"You mean, George, he wants some sucker for a blind date? Not interested! Anyway, why don't *you* take him up on it?"

"I'm already fixed up for tonight Alf, but I know that you haven't got anything planned."

"Look, George, you know there is someone special for me at home. I would feel I was betraying her."

"Nonsense Alf, it's only a blind date after all. She won't be expecting you to propose! Go on, Alf, it will be a break for you, a change from looking at my ugly mug."

Reluctantly I did go along with this guy called Alan Dobbs. We met the girls in the cafe meeting place in Hythe.

Sandra turned out to be my blind date. She was an extremely nice girl, very cute. All four of us decided to go to the local cinema, the Roxie, I believe it was called.

During the walk from the cafe to the cinema, Sandra explained that she felt guilty because she already had a boyfriend serving in the Royal Signals, out in Singapore. "Sandra," I said, "strikes me that me and you are both in the same boat! I too have someone special back home, so don't feel guilty. There is nothing wrong if we both enjoy each other's company for one night." She gave me a dazzling smile and said, "Come on Alf, let's enjoy the film!"

"Why not, Sandra," I smiled, "and we might just enjoy an ice cream together too."

After the film, Alan and Brenda, Sandra's friend, split up with us. Apparently Brenda lived nearby, but Sandra needed to catch a bus.

"Come on Sandra," I said, "let me walk you to the bus station, or would you like a drink or something first?"

"Better not, Alf, don't want to be getting home too late. Look, Alf, I have really enjoyed tonight! Let's repeat it just one more time before you go back to Germany. It's made me realise tonight, Alf, just how lonely I have been since Peter went abroad."

"Sure Sandra, I'll get in contact with you through Alan."

Sandra's bus had now pulled into the bay. Just before Sandra stepped onto the bus, I gave her a small kiss on the cheek. "Until next week then," I smiled, and then the bus pulled off.

I was left standing there, feeling guiltier than ever. Don't be stupid, I said to myself, there is nothing wrong in enjoying someone else's company. Perhaps it was because I was missing Maureen and I was feeling lonely too.

The following morning it was more instruction on wind and elevation tables. These tables made an immense difference to a soldier's accuracy. Plus, we would have to teach these tables ourselves when we got back to Germany.

Thursday morning arrived. While George and I were looking on part one orders, we noticed my name was up there.

"Of all the rotten luck, George," I complained, "they have gone and put me on flipping guard duty, guarding the ruddy armoury of all places!"

George turned to me. "That's tough Alf, but there is a story about that particular armoury. Apparently one night the ruddy I.R.A. tried an unsuccessful attempt of breaking into it; hence the ruddy place as been guarded ever since. When are you on?"

"Saturday night, George."

We decided to ask our instructor to see just what was involved.

"Well, it's like this; you will be locked in the armoury room from 20.00 hrs until 08.00 hrs the following morning. You will be issued with a rifle and five live rounds of ammunition. If, and only if, you should come under attack, you will ring the guardroom and get authority form the orderly officer, before you load your rifle." He then smiled and, looking directly at me, said, "If it was me, Corporal, and I had come under attack, I would load my rifle and I would have one up the damned spout—then I would phone the orderly officer—that's if I was under attack!"

That Thursday evening, George and I sat in the NAAFI when Alan came in and joined us.

"Hi Alf, fancy joining us again this Saturday night? There's a dance on in Hythe?"

"Sorry, Alan, no can do. I've drawn the short straw. I'm on guard duty this Saturday."

"Oh, hell! What about Sunday then?"

"Sure, that will be okay."

"Great, there's another dance on Sunday at the Empress. It's just that Sandra—you remember the blind date?—well, she's been asking about you."

"Tell her I'm sorry about Saturday but I'll be there for sure on Sunday."

"Hang on," George burst out, "what's this all about, Sandra asking about you?"

"Don't be silly, we had a great time last time and we want to repeat it; there's no harm in it, George."

However, when Sunday arrived and I saw Sandra again, I'm sure my heart skipped a beat—she looked absolutely stunning! She wore a brown dress with a white collar and cuffs. Her shoes were brown and white. It all matched her soft brown hair and her lovely brown eyes, which seemed to light up when we saw each other again.

When we got on the dance floor, I held her close. I could smell her perfume and feel the softness of her hair as it brushed my cheek. It was as if we were the only two on the dance floor at that moment. The only words we spoke were to tell each other how much we'd missed one another.

Now I felt guilty but how can you help your feelings? It wasn't supposed to be like this. She looked at me with those soft brown eyes and said, "It is just as well that you are going back to Germany next week, Alf, because I think I am beginning to fall for you."

"Let's just enjoy this evening, Sandra, because tonight belongs to us. It's wonderful just being here with you"—and I held her a little tighter. It was like some fairytale romance, not real like, but like some wonderful dream we both knew would have to end that night.

Again I walked Sandra back to the bus. This time Sandra said, "I'll always remember tonight, will you?"

"Always," I replied.

"Just kiss me properly, Alf, and then go—don't look back, please."

The following morning at breakfast, George said, "Well, this is our last week on the course. Next Friday we'll be given our grades. Wonder how well we will have done? There seems so much to remember."

"An average grading will do me, George. Anything above that will be a bonus."

When Friday arrived, we were all assembled in the cookhouse. The major and the sergeant major came in. "I will read out the results in alphabetical order."

Everybody must have been nervous waiting for those all-important results that morning. George's name was first to be called. "Corporal Briggs, 'B'—what a result, George, well done!"

Eventually my name came up. Corporal Cartwright—'B'.

"Wow, George, I'll feel a bit happier packing tomorrow—what a result!"

Chapter Sixteen

We arrived back in Herford at 14.15 hrs on the Sunday. Again transport had been laid on for us to take us back to camp. As the K5 drew through the camp gates, the only light we could see was coming from the guardroom. The rest of the camp was in darkness. The orderly sergeant came out. "Transport in the form of a Land Rover has been laid on to take you two to Belefield. The whole ruddy column has moved there since you two left. Now you are here we can pack up ourselves."

Belefield was only about thirty-five kilometres from Herford and the journey was much more comfortable in the Land Rover. We pulled up outside the new column training wing. It was now about 16.30 hrs. The training wing reminded me of the old spider huts we had had in the basic training. Sergeant Major Fox was apparently the acting training wing officer, until a new one arrived. We hadn't had much to do with the Sergeant Major before; he had been with 'B' company.

The Sergeant Major said, "There is a new batch of recruits in the training wing at the moment from England; they are about halfway through the course. The training staff has been struggling, to say the least. They will be real glad to have some reinforcements."

Then Corporal Warboys appeared. "Come on, lads, and I'll show you both your new billet. You can sort all your kit out. RSM French wants to see you both in the morning first thing; you will both be going in front of the Colonel in the morning. So you will both be polishing and pressing tonight—you know what a stickler the R.S.M. is, lads!"

"Great! And all I wanted to do tonight was to knock off and spend an hour down the NAAFI."

"Look, you two," said Corporal Warboys, "we've got a staff room here. Come on down and have a coffee before you do anything—and look, everyone around here calls me Curly."

"Okay Curly, lead the way!" I said as George and I entered the staff room.

I was in for another surprise. Seated in the corner, smoking his pipe, was Jim! When he saw me he jumped up.

"Great to see you again, Alf!"—and we shook hands.

"Look George, this is Jim, my old buddy from 'C' platoon, Are you here for the duration, Jim?"

"It certainly looks that way, Alf, until the completion of my National Service next June."

"When did you get your stripe, Jim?"

"Oh, it was just after you and George went on your course.

They don't usually like to give us National Servicemen promotion. It's because they wanted me in the training wing."

"Look, its teatime now—leave your kit, lads, until after you have eaten. Come on, me and Curly will show you both the way. It's a bit of a trail to the cookhouse from the training wing."

The four of us set off.

During the meal, George asked, "What's the story of Foxy in the training wing?"

Curly said, "We believe that it is only until Christmas; then we get ourselves a brand new training wing officer. At the end of the day it is us who really run the training wing, not Foxy. Foxy is just a sort of figurehead, so to speak, plus he never really bothers us."

"Oh, remember sergeant Hardcastle and Wiles?" George grinned. "Well, they have both gone back into the companies now. Now we are blessed with two new ones. Sergeant Holmes and Breck, and they are both great guys. We help them out from time to time by taking the men onto the parade ground for drill instruction. You two will soon get the hang of it!"

The following morning, George and I set off for the HQ. We had been instructed to report there for 09.00 hrs. The time was now 08.50 hrs. As we got close to the HQ building, the R.S.M. came around the corner and we followed him inside the building.

"Stand there, corporals! How have you both done at the Hythe? What grades have you both got?"

We both spoke together: "'B' grades, Sir!"

The R.S.M. looked at us. "Grade 'B'—no one has ever come back from Hythe with those grades! Bloody well done, well done!"—and he gave us both a hearty slap on our backs.

After checking with the colonel, he marched us in. The colonel was looking down reading through the reports on his desk. After a while he looked up. His face was beaming. "Jolly good show, men, jolly good show! These reports are excellent. You are qualified in all small arms and qualified to oversee range work when you hold the rank. Again, well done! March them out, Regimental Sergeant Major!"

Once outside the colonel's office, the R.S.M. told us to report back to the training wing.

Curly met us just outside the training wing. "Come on lads, you'll need a cuppa after that! We've got about forty-five minutes before the recruits come off the square. We've got a double period before dinner. Wind and Elevation tables, that will take us up to 11.30 hrs and give us an extended dinner break. I think that once you've both settled in you will both enjoy the training wing, plus there is another bonus for us—we don't get any duties like guard duty or orderly corporal duties. The R.S.M. believes that his instructors can't instruct to the best of their abilities if they have been up all night."

"What was that, George? No more weekend guard duties? Now, that *is* a bonus!"

Walking into that lecture room for the very first time was a trifle daunting, to say the least. There were twelve pairs of eyes staring back at me. Twelve young men were looking to me for words of wisdom.

All those young lads would be tested at the end of the course, for their ability to instruct, to a small degree. Just like George and I had been tested. However, the first few moments from entering into that lecture room, it felt strange. But only for the first few moments from entering, then the lessons seemed to flow. At the end of those first two lessons, the young men seemed quite impressed. After the lesson one young man approached me and said, "Corporal, we never learnt the things you have shown until this morning. I am finding the weapon training really interesting." As he was speaking, he reminded me of myself. How keen I was when I first came through the training wing!

"What is your name, driver?"

"Roberts, Corporal. Peter Roberts."

"Are you a National Serviceman, Peter Roberts?"

"Yes, Corporal."

"Well, it is my job to make your short stay in the army as interesting as possible. You can come and see me any time in the evenings, if you are not sure on any point and I will clarify it for you."

"Thank you Corporal—I will certainly do that!"

Looking at my watch, it was exactly 11.33 hrs. Most of the recruits had now disappeared into their quarters. I made my way to the staff room. George hadn't arrived yet but Jim and Curly were there.

"How did you get along, Alf?"

"Great, Curly, great. A little daunting, those first minutes, but they soon passed. I quite enjoyed it."

"The first day is always the worst. In a few weeks from now it will be like falling off a log. The recruits come through here once every twelve weeks. In between that we instruct on 1 and 2 drill courses and section commanders courses. The first time on the parade ground we will all go on and put the recruits through the passing out parade. This way, Alf, you and George will get the hang of the procedure, just what is involved, like. At least each passing out parade is exactly the same."

That first week in the training wing just seemed to fly by. Curly always went home at the weekend, lucky blighter. He had married a German girl and they had a little girl of about three years old. His house was detached and in its own grounds. Curly, it would seem, had fallen lucky. His wife had bought and paid for the house before she had met him.

George, the dark horse, had apparently struck up a relationship with Blondie from the NAAFI while we were in Herford and had kept in touch with her through letter writing while we were on the course in Hythe. This weekend, he had planned to see her.

Jim and I thought he was a bloody fool. Blondie was married but her husband was in prison. We tried to tell him that he was just stirring up trouble for himself but he wouldn't listen.

"Got any plans, Jim?"

"Yes, I'd like to go into Bielefeld this Saturday, Alf. Haven't been in yet. Apparently it's much larger than Herford and there is a decent YMCA there. Fancy coming along, Alf?"

"Sure, why not."

That Saturday morning, Jim and I caught the bus just outside the camp gates. The bus only took us about two kilometres and then we changed onto a connecting tram. The trams looked as though they had been running since before the war. The whole journey took only about thirty-five minutes from the camp.

As we stepped off the tram, we both looked about us. In front of us was a huge complex of roads, all joining at this point. "Come on, Alf, there seems to be a subway over there." Jim was right about the subway. It led down and under the mass of roads above. In fact, it was the only way to get to the other side and into the City. But to our amazement, there was a complete shopping centre underground. We had never seen anything like it back home. Once through the subway, it brought us out to the main shopping area. We must have been walking around for about an hour. They even had a

Woolworths there! Eventually we found the YMCA—it was right in the centre, and somewhere where we could speak our native tongue.

If one could afford it, you could phone home from there. But that ruled Jim and me out. Plus, I didn't know anyone back home who had a phone. Jim said that that facility was just for the rich and famous.

After we'd both had a tea and a cake, we decided to head back to camp.

"What do you think of Bielefeld, Alf?"

"It's okay. I guess it's an improvement on Herford. Plenty of choice in shops, I suppose, if you're looking to buy some presents."

The following week the recruits would be taking their first passing out parade. There was a drill course coming up which would consist mostly of N.C.O.'s but there was a full week's break between the two courses.

We were all seated in the staff room when George said, "Curly, is this a free week?"

"Sure," replied Curly, "but we pretend to be busy."

"Like doing what?" I said.

"Well, for one thing, Alf, this drill course that's coming up, we need to work out a training program for it. Besides that, we sit in the office and push a few papers around. If we go down into the camp, we carry a millboard and look important. No one ever questions us. Surprisingly, we seem to get respect wherever we go."

Christmas 1957 was approaching rapidly. We were now into December. Since George and I had arrived back from Hythe, numerous courses had passed through the training wing. It surprised me just how much those Hythe instructors had drilled into us. Things kept coming back to me. Now I could instruct on any weapons without making out lesson plans, something that I used to rely on.

Sergeant Major Fox had invited us all to come around to his married quarters for a meal. That was pretty decent of him and his wife. It was Boxing Day and she did us all proud. But on Christmas morning it was traditional in the army for the sergeants to bring everyone a cup of tea and whisky in bed. Mind you, this only happened on Christmas Day!

It was straight after Christmas when George came around to me and Jim. George sat down on the bed, looked at us and said, "I'm in one hell of a mess, lads."

"What is it, George?"

"Nobody can help, Alf. Remember Blondie, lads? Well, she's pregnant and her husband is due out of prison in three weeks' time!"

"Hell!" Jim retorted, "You *are* in a mess!"

George went on to say, "That's only part of it, lads. I've also been seeing this young lass from Bielefeld. She's also told me *she's* pregnant!"

"Bloody hell, George! You *have* been busy!"

"There's more! During my last leave, I went and slept with my sister-in-law."

"Don't tell us *she's* pregnant as well!"

"I know I've been a bloody fool and I don't know which way to turn. She's gone and told my brother that she loves me and that I'm the only real man she's ever slept with! Now my brother and father have said they will be waiting for me when I get demobbed. I was going to find out if I could join the merchant navy from here."

"Now you are grabbing at straws," said Jim. "When are you

due to be demobbed?"

"The seventeenth of next month."

"We wouldn't wish to be in your shoes for anything, but we will try to cover for you as much as we can until your release."

When George left us, I looked at Jim. "What about that then? Jim, when I was in Hythe, I met this young girl. We went out together a few times and we were immediately drawn to each other. In a short space of time we had started to fall in love. We both felt bad, but we couldn't help our feelings. We knew it couldn't last because we didn't want anyone getting hurt, but we treasured the time we had together. All this time and I still feel guilty, Jim, and no, we didn't sleep together—I respected her. But George is in a class all on his own. No morals at all—he likes to play the field!"

"But if you remember, Alf, we *did* try and warn him, told him he was playing with fire—but he took no notice of us."

George's demob date came and went. However, he did manage to evade Blondie's husband and the parents of the young girl from Bielefeld.

But that still left his father and brother to face when he finally reached home.

"In May, Alf, I'll be off—it will be my National Service completed!"

"You're going to be missed, Jim. You and me go back a long way. Before the Suez caper. The training wing won't be the same. I've heard through the grapevine that we are getting a replacement for George. A full corporal from the training wing in Minden. Curly originally came from Minden. Anyway, the idea is that I train him up like and prepare him for Hythe."

The following week was a free week between courses. Curly

and I had set up a table tennis table in the spare lecture room. It was on Tuesday morning when Curly and I were engrossed in a game. Jim had gone to the staff room to make us all a brew. The next thing we knew was, Jim had come back into the room, followed by our new training wing officer. Both Curly and I snapped to attention.

The training wing officer stood there smiling. "Carry on men, I'll play the winner!"

Chapter Seventeen

"My name is Lieutenant Dick Leeming, and I am your new training wing officer. I am quite informal, lads; you will find me easy to get along with. In the confines of four walls I'd like you all to address me as Dick. However, outside it will have to be Lieutenant Leeming. Now who's going to show me the ropes?"

Everyone seemed to look at me, so I stepped forward. "My name is Corporal Cartwright, Sir"

"What's your first name, Corporal Cartwright?"

"Alf, Sir."

"Then like I said, it will be Alf in this office. This first name arrangement goes both ways," said Dick

We all took an instant liking to Dick; we'd never experienced having a training wing officer quite like him.

That afternoon I spent several hours in the office with Dick, taking him through all the various courses that came through the training wing. "HQ will negotiate directly with you, Dick. You can then let us know of any new courses coming in. The course reports at the end of each course are simple. Each instructor takes notes on a daily basis, so that at the end of the course, it is simpler to get an accurate report on every soldier. The instructors change around at the end of the course for grading the men. Curly or I will finally check each report before they are brought into the office. Then they are passed on to Lance Corporal Lawson—that's Jim. He types everything out—he's a wizard on the old typewriter. All the instructors sign their respective report and finally you sign each one, Dick. Once they are all completed they are finally distributed to their respective companies. Wednesday evening is the traditional bull night, for your Thursday inspection. One of us will accompany you on the rounds. We do tend to be a bit hard on then but they know the score, and don't expect anything less."

Dick grinned at me. "We've all been there, Alf, at one time or another."

"Don't worry about the course schedules. Dick, me and Curly always work out the lesson plans for each course. Monday morning is the start of a three weeks course. A new batch of recruits is arriving from England. The poor blighters are coming here believing they will be joining a working unit.

"On Sunday evening, four of us will go down to the station in Bielefeld to meet them off the train. When I first arrived in Germany, I experienced this myself. We've decided to throw in a couple of route marches this time around, Dick, but it will be early, before breakfast. We don't want to disrupt their training programme. Look, Dick, we've got a new N.C.O. joining us this weekend. I believe his name is Corporal Armstrong. He is being sent down form Minden. He has, I'm told, had quite a bit of experience from the training wing there. However, they want me to groom him for the course at Hythe. They're sending him there on the 5th April. Shall we take a break, Dick, and I'll organise coffee or tea if you prefer?"

Over a cup of tea, Dick revealed to me that he was getting married in September. "Are you getting married over here Dick?" I asked.

"Yes, my future good lady will be coming over from Jersey. Now then, I would like you and the other N.C.O.'s to attend my wedding, to act as ushers and finally wait on the tables at the reception. Of course, you will have to wear your number one dress."

"Dick, I doubt very much that any other lads have been issued with any blues."

"That's something you can check out for me, Alf. Just find out how many will be required and leave it to me, I'll organise the uniforms." He smiled. "Nothing must go wrong on my big day."

Monday morning arrived. We all had decided to include Corporal Armstrong in the first route march. His first name turned out to be Pete. Myself, Curly and Pete were standing in the corridor and the time was 05.00 hrs.

"Come on, let's get these sleeping beauties out of bed! Come on, you horrible lot!" We were all screaming: "Get yourselves out of bed. If anyone is caught in bed in two minutes, they will be on a charge. All of you will be outside on parade in full battle dress by 05.30 hrs. We are taking you all on a small route march before breakfast!" I remember that particular morning well. We sort of moved out of camp silently so as not to wake the whole camp. It had just started to get light.

Outside the camp we quickly increased the pace. We covered a distance of about five miles in just over an hour.

It was 06.45 when we were standing outside the training wing again. Straight after breakfast, the two drill sergeants had taken the men down onto the parade ground for the first two periods. It meant we had a free period right until after NAAFI break.

"What do you think about it all so far, Pete?"

"Is it always this hectic on Monday mornings?"

"What do you mean, Pete?"

"What do you think, these ruddy marches of course!"

We all laughed.

"The route marches are only on Monday mornings, plus we are going to take turns. Look, Pete, this special treatment is only reserved for the new recruits, fresh out of training from dear old Blighty!"

"Well, that's a bloody relief!" Pete burst out.

"Has anyone offered to take Dick for a cup of tea this morning?"

"I have," said Curly. "Oh, and by the way, he was looking for you earlier on, Alf. Better trot down and see what it's all about."

Entering the office, Dick looked up from his paperwork. "Ah, just the man, Alf. The RSM would like to see you."

"Know what it's about, Dick?"

"Not a clue, but you had better get down there. I have covered for you, and I've told him that you are fully engaged until after 10.30 hrs. He said he would expect you then."

"Thanks Dick, I'll call on my way back from the NAAFI."

Standing outside the RSM's office that morning, I wondered what he wanted with me. Knocking on the door I heard the RSM'S voice bark: "Enter!" Once inside his office, I stood rigidly to attention. The RSM demanded the ultimate respect. Anything short of that and you felt he would eat you alive.

"Stand at ease, Corporal Cartwright. On the 7th April, I am starting the first of my number three drill courses. It will be my course designed especially for senior ranks—sergeants. I will give them instruction on the parade ground in ceremonial drill. You, Corporal Cartwright, will instruct them in the lecture room to cover the weapons side. You will give them, during the course, each senior rank three lessons. I will choose any one of these three lessons at the end of the course—to test their ability to instruct."

"Sir, there is a section commanders' course starting on the same date."

"Look, corporal, I will make sure that you have a copy of my schedule—then you will be able to juggle between the two courses. However, my course must always be given your first priority. You, Corporal, will be responsible for my senior ranks. Don't ever delegate, Corporal Cartwright—only you will give my senior ranks instructions."

The 7th April came around very quickly. I remember that very first morning. I entered the lecture room which I'd prepared earlier. The 3.5 rocket launcher was set on a trestle table. Twelve sergeants were staring back at me, all relying on me to get them through this course. At first, just for the first few minutes, it felt daunting, but that feeling soon passed. Two of them I knew well. The others were obviously selected from different companies. A few I did recognise but only by sight. However, sitting there was Sergeant Wiles, my old drill instructor, and he obviously needed my input to get through this course. Next to him was Sergeant Williams, our old enemy from 'C' platoon. Jim would be pleased!

After that lesson I couldn't wait to see Jim's face and break the good news.

"Jim! Do you remember Williams? Sergeant Williams—that is, from 'C' platoon?"

"Of course, Alf, that man made our lives hell!"

"But do you remember your wish, Jim! You said one day Williams would come unstuck and when that happened, you would like to be there?"

"Yes, yes, Alf, go on!"

"Well Jim, he hasn't exactly come unstuck, but he has come up here on a course. He's been in my lecture room this very morning. *We* are in control now, Jim! Isn't it bloody marvellous!"

"Yes Alf! Don't make it easy for him! Why not give him some difficult lessons for the RSM to choose from?"

As bad as Williams had been with Jim and me, I would still get him through the course, because that was my job.

"You will be leaving us next month, Jim. I'll bet you can't wait to get back with your good wife. We'll all miss you, especially me, Jim. It will be my turn next February. That's if I don't sign on again."

The night before Jim's leaving, we all took him down to the NAAFI for a party. All the lads from 'C' platoon turned up. It was a little something we would all remember.

Dick told us that the N.C.O.'s course was coming up on the second week in June. Included on the course would be several cooks from the cookhouse. This turned out to be very beneficial on our part. The cooks were just like everyone else. Dreading the thought of coming up to the training wing, they tried to get into our good books before the course started, by giving us tins of bacon, tins of sausages and cheese. So now instead of going to the NAAFI in the morning, we would have a fry up in the staff room. Dick never bothered us; even he got himself a sandwich. However, the arrangement wasn't entirely risk free, so we had a look out. One of us would stand outside the staff room and keep watch, just in case someone entered the training wing.

Just as fate would have it, one morning the RSM was standing at the entrance of the training wing, with his nose in the air and sniffing. "Bloody hell!" said Curly, "It's the RSM!" Windows were thrown open, the stove was turned off and everything was bunged into the lockers.

"Quick, lads, keep calm and quiet. I'll try to divert him." Some of the lads jumped out of the window and worked their way to the rear of the building, to make out they had entered from one of the other training blocks. I did manage to divert the RSM into the office where Dick was, and retreated, leaving him talking to Dick.

Dick's wedding was now looming. He had managed to get all of us N.C.O.'s our number one dress. These were our blues. Myself, I wasn't too keen on them. The stripes or chevrons were woven in like a gold braid. No, I wasn't too keen at all.

Pete Armstrong had come back from Hythe now and another N.C.O. had joined us to replace Jim—a corporal, Derek Smith. "Pete, I'll leave Derek to you; check him out please. He does need to be compliant. We have another section commando course coming up, plus I have another number three drill course for the RSM coming up. He must be something, like, because he's being sent to Hythe too. You can give me a hand to train him up. It does mean, though, that Dick will have to muster some more number one dresses up, if he wants us all to attend his wedding."

In Germany, we had a radio station for the troops—The British Forces Network, and you could send in requests. We all wrote a request for Dick on the eve of his wedding. We asked for the record called 'I'm getting married in the morning' and we signed it, from all the boys of the column training wing. The wedding went great and afterwards we all waited on at his reception. Dick told me to tell the lads to have a few drinks on him—as long as we all kept upright!

Plus, he asked us to stay back after everyone else had left to have a celebratory drink with him and his lovely new bride. Then, just before we were about to leave, he handed each one of us a bottle of champagne. Yes, Dick was one of the best officers anyone could wish to serve under—a real gent.

Christmas would soon be upon us again and so would my release. I had decided to leave the army in February. After all, I had only signed on for that extra year.

Furthermore, I didn't think Maureen would have adjusted to army life.

♣

Maureen and I are now coming up to our fiftieth wedding anniversary. It's been more than fifty years since my National Service days. Fifty years since the recruitment sergeant pressed that shiny new shilling into the palm of my hand, saying, "That's the Queen's shilling, lad!" It all seems just like yesterday.

When I close my eyes, I can picture in my mind's eye, all their faces, from those early days in training at Yeovil. The same is true of all my friends I met in Germany, like Jim, Curly the training wing officer, and Dick—Dick who gave us all a bottle of champagne on his wedding day. The list goes on and on.

But most of all, what I did learn from the army was comradeship—true comradeship.

That is something that has stayed with me throughout all these years.

"A BAND OF BROTHERS!"

THE END

About the Author

Alfred Cartwright was born on the 18th April 1938, in the small village of Thornton, near Bradford, in West Yorkshire. His education was at a modest Secondary Modern School.

He enlisted in the British Army on the 8th of February 1956, and served for three years until the 8th February 1959. He was married to Maureen on the 28th February 1959.

In April 1986, the author needed heart by-pass surgery, but with Maureen's constant care he survived through those years. Now he has found time to put pen to paper, a process he finds very relaxing.